jabberrock

Raymond Obstfeld
and
Patricia Fitzgerald

an owl book | henry holt and company | new york

The Ultimate Book of Rock 'n' Roll Quotations

JABBERROCK

Henry Holt and Company, Inc.
Publishers since 1866
115 West 18th Street
New York, New York 10011

Henry Holt® is a registered
trademark of Henry Holt and Company, Inc.

Library of Congress Cataloging-in-Publication Data
Obstfeld, Raymond, date.
Jabberrock: the ultimate book of rock 'n' roll quotations /
Raymond Obstfeld and Patricia Fitzgerald.
p.   cm.
"An owl book."
ISBN 0-8050-4887-1 (pbk.: alk. paper)
1. Rock music—Quotations, maxims, etc.   2. Rock musicians—
Quotations.   I. Fitzgerald, Patricia.   II. Title.
PN6084.R62027   1997   97-11880
781.66—dc21   CIP

Henry Holt books are available for special promotions and
premiums. For details contact: Director, Special Markets.

First Edition 1997

Designed by Debbie Glasserman

Printed in the United States of America
All first editions are printed on acid-free paper. ∞

10 9 8 7 6 5 4 3 2 1

for ceebs, our patron saint.

—patricia fitzgerald

c o n t e n t s

ix

introduction:
it's only
rock 'n' roll

There are about a gadzillion books on rock 'n' roll and they all start by telling you how important rock is in the history of the universe. We figure you already know that. Sure, rock changed the world—and it did so just when the world most needed changing. The country had barely emerged from a nasty world war that left everyone feeling battered, bruised, and very uncertain about their future. Although the A-bomb was stored in the closet, it was still on people's minds. A new generation was growing up with the uneasy knowledge that one nut case with an itchy finger and a caffeine buzz could indeed destroy the world. (Or as the Kingston Trio sang it: "And you can be certain that some lovely day / Someone will set the bomb off, and we will all be blown away.") It was like living with a violent parent who only beat you when he was drunk—you always kept one eye on the liquor cabinet. All these war-weary survivors wanted now was a little peace and quiet on the home front—to enjoy the fruits of their suffering and sacrifice. For them this Utopia meant a world with as little conflict as possible—which translated into everyone acting, dressing, and looking alike. The sooner everyone resembled the pod people from *Invasion of the Body Snatchers,* the sooner we'd all be happy. In other words, it was the Fifties.

Rock changed all that. Elvis, Jerry Lee Lewis, Buddy Holly, the Shangri-las, and the rest of the pioneers were belting out the kind of music that gave release to the pent-up frustrations of moving obediently through adolescence. While rock's first offshoots sprang from the roots of black music, it quickly spread to white middle-class teens as a kind of secret handshake among America's Underground Resistance: teenagers fighting the nameless, faceless Social Expectations of living in Podland Mall. Rock made fun of those expectations. It made fun of its own fans. It even made fun of itself. The key attitude was fun. And it gave a loud pounding voice to the teen emotions and passions that so far had been dismissed, ignored, or trivialized by Them. However, once you give people a voice, you can't shut them up again.

Rock may have started as nothing more than heckling from the back row of society's bleachers, but it quickly grew to a unified voice amplified by AM radio stations and wacky disc jockeys across the country. The problem is, once you've got a voice, you've got to think of something to say. There's only so many times you can rhapsodize over being sweet sixteen or itsy-bitsy, teenie-weenie yellow polka dot bikinis. So, as the world changed, that voice changed too, losing its adolescent squeak in order to include a larger, more complex world. That voice was no longer just a cry of defiance or youthful *angst,* it was also a litany of opinions and demands. When Bob Dylan sang "Blowin' in the Wind" or John Lennon performed "Imagine," they undoubtedly called more people to political action than any President's State of the Union Address. During the craziness of the Vietnam War, rock 'n' roll became the national anthem of protest. And when there were other social ills to bring to public attention, rock spoke up first: Marvin Gaye with "What's Goin' On," Cat Stevens with "Where Do the Children Play?" and even Elvis with "In the Ghetto." In the end, these voices were always about passion—about people caring what happened to themselves, to each other, to their world.

We've collected those voices here. The writers, singers, producers, and musicians who reveal to us the view from inside the belly of the beast: the lessons, agonies, triumphs, defeats, insights, feuds, foolishness, horrors, tragedies, and strangeness of being part of that Voice. Their personal lives were as turbulent as the times they sang about: Janis Joplin, Mick Jagger, Kurt Cobain, Jimi Hendrix, Elvis Presley, The Beatles, Tupac Shakur. To find these quotes, we researched for over three years, digging through biographies, autobiographies, magazines, newspapers, radio and TV interviews, even the Internet—just about every source that provided a platform for rockers to speak from their hearts. Most of the time we were able to attach a date to the quote, thereby allowing the reader to put an utterance in historical context. In some cases, we've included several quotes by the same person on the same subject, but spoken over a period of years. This allows for some insight into how opinions change. (Mick Jagger had to reconsider what he said in the Sixties: "I'd rather be dead than singing 'Satisfaction' when I'm forty-five.")

John Lennon said that the best rock 'n' roll is "primitive energy and has no bullshit." This is true not only of the music, but also of the rock 'n' roll Attitude. It is that attitude that these quotes reflect, taken from a passionate group of artists who know what it's like to struggle in anonymity, rocket to fame and fortune, crash and burn, fight to change the world—and ultimately describe that marvelous journey for us with primitive energy and no bullshit.

jabberrock

Rock 'n' Roll

chapter one

SPONTANEOUSLY COMBUSTIBLE

s h a k e ,   r a t t l e ,   &   r o l l

 **like rock 'n' roll, and I don't like much else.** —JOHN LENNON (1940–1980)

I just heard rock 'n' roll in my head so fucking loud that I couldn't ignore it. —NEIL YOUNG, 1988

Of course I wanted to work in the rock 'n' roll tradition. I didn't know any other tradition existed. —PATTI SMITH, 1976

Rock 'n' roll music, if you like it, if you feel it, you can't help but move to it. That's what happens to me. I can't help it. —ELVIS PRESLEY (1935–1977)

I think of what I do first as making music, but I also think of myself as a rock singer. —BARRY MANILOW

If you don't have sex and you don't do drugs, your rock 'n' roll better be awfully good. —ABBIE HOFFMAN (1936–1989), left-wing political activist and member of the Chicago Seven, 1988

Take the drugs away and there's more time for sex and rock 'n' roll. —STEVEN TYLER, of Aerosmith

You can be organized and still rock. It's not really a prerequisite in this field to be a heroin addict—that's a misconception. —MARK BRYAN, of Hootie and the Blowfish, 1995

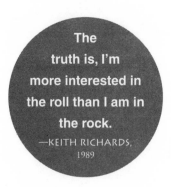

The truth is, I'm more interested in the roll than I am in the rock.

—KEITH RICHARDS, 1989

Energy is what you need in rock 'n' roll. Energy and three chords.

—MICK JAGGER

Rock 'n' roll's a man's job, little brother.

—FREDDIE MERCURY (1946–1991), of
Queen, to Michael Jackson, 1983

When musicians interact or space out and do their own thing but somehow it works, they call it jazz. If you play it loud and it has more aggressive guitar, then they call it rock 'n' roll.

—EDDIE VAN HALEN

I've always said that hard rock, or big rock music, is simply folk music delivered at high velocity. Shot from guns. We simply reflect what we see in newspapers, magazines, what you've lived and breathed before. —DAVID LEE ROTH

When you make rock 'n' roll, the more you think, the more you stink. . . . Rock 'n' roll is fire. It has to do with how much you can thumb your nose at the world.

—DAVID BRIGGS (1944–1995), coproducer
of 17 Neil Young albums, 1991

True rock 'n' roll has no form, it's nebulous. And if rock 'n' roll happens to sometimes also be a rebellion or a reaction to something, that is never its primary purpose. The main purpose of rock 'n' roll is celebration of the self.

—DARYL HALL, of Hall & Oates, 1987

The rock 'n' roll spirit is not survival. Of course the people who play rock 'n' roll should survive. But the essence of that rock 'n' roll spirit, to me, is that it's better to burn out really bright than it is to sort of decay off into infinity. . . . Rock 'n' roll doesn't look that far ahead. Rock 'n' roll is right now. What's happening right this second. Is it bright? Or is it dim because it's waiting for tomorrow?

—NEIL YOUNG, 1982

Rock 'n' roll for me is not necessarily an end in itself. It's a means to some other end, to trying to improve the world and the community.

—DON HENLEY

Rock won't eliminate your problems. But it will let you sort of dance all over them. —PETE TOWNSHEND

For our style, it has always been less is more and that rock 'n' roll was supposed to be fun. —JOEY RAMONE, of the Ramones

Rock 'n' roll is supposed to be fun. You remember fun, don'tcha? You're supposed to enjoy it. —JOHNNY ROTTEN, of the Sex Pistols, 1978

> Not even boot camp is as tough as being in rock 'n' roll. —PATTI SMITH

That's what rock 'n' roll is for me, a kind of rebellious thing, getting away from authority figures, getting laid maybe, doing drugs at some point.

—SLASH, of Guns N' Roses, 1986

Rock is all about writing your own script; it's all about pioneering.

—COURTNEY LOVE, of Hole, 1995

Rock 'n' roll is like a drug. I don't take very much rock 'n' roll, but when I do rock 'n' roll, I fuckin' do it. But I don't want to do it all the time 'cause it'll kill me. When you're singing and playing rock 'n' roll, you're on the leading edge of yourself. You're tryin' to vibrate, tryin' to make something happen. It's like there's somethin' alive and exposed. —NEIL YOUNG, 1985

Rock 'n' roll is . . . about spirit, and I think the true spirit of rock 'n' roll is somewhere close to abandonment.
—BONO, 1987

Rock 'n' roll starts between the legs and goes through the heart, then to the head. As long as it does those three things, it's a great rock song. —JOHN MELLENCAMP

So, what is it about this rock 'n' roll? Well, it's the thing that shakes you out of your marriage. It's the thing that disarranges your kidneys. It's what kills your liver. It's what sells McDonald's. It's a gathering place. —IGGY POP

The best stuff is primitive energy and has no bullshit. [Rock 'n' roll] gets through to you; it got through to me, the only thing to get through to me of all the things that were happening when I was 15. Rock 'n' roll then was real; everything else was unreal. The thing about rock 'n' roll, good rock 'n' roll—whatever good means and all that shit—is that it's real, and realism gets through to you despite yourself. You recognize something in it which is true, like all true art.
—JOHN LENNON (1940–1980)

Rock can be seen as one attempt to break out of this dead and soulless universe and reassert the universe of magic[k]. —WILLIAM BURROUGHS, author

[Rock 'n' roll] is a living art, and it is undergoing constant reevaluation and change. Which makes it far more interesting than, say, painting or any of the plastic arts.
—DAVID BOWIE

Rock is art and a million other things as well: It's an indescribable form of communication and entertainment combined, and it's a two-way thing with very complex but real feedback processes.
—PETE TOWNSHEND

People who are looking for art in rock 'n' roll or pop are looking for something that either doesn't or shouldn't exist.

—BILLY JOEL, 1980

[Rock 'n' roll] changed the world. It reshaped the way people think. You can build a wall to stop people, but eventually the music will cross that wall. That's the beautiful thing about music—there's no defense against it. I mean, look at Joshua and fuckin' Jericho—made mincemeat of that joint. A few trumpets, you know?

—KEITH RICHARDS, 1987

The function of rock 'n' roll is to annoy parents.

—BOB MERLIS, Warner Brothers publicity executive

Rock is more like the blues, which have been telling the truth for so many years, but for so long only spoke to blacks. Rock deals with sadness, bummers, fear, despair, adversity, desperation, as well as sex, sensuality, highs, and super-highs. The straight world tends to like escapist entertainment, the hip world accepts more pain and thus more reality. If the "new culture" [of rock 'n' roll] is anything, it is a movement toward a greater personal reality.

—CHARLES REICH, Yale professor and rock critic/biographer, 1972

Rock 'n' roll music is the energy center for all sorts of changes revolving rapidly around us: social, political, cultural, however you want to describe them. The fact is for many of us who've grown up since World War II, rock 'n' roll provided the first revolutionary insight into who we are and where we are in this country: our first discovery that behind the plasticized myth of what we had been told was the United States, behind that Eisenhower–Walt Disney–Doris Day facade was (damn!) a real America: funky, violent, deeply divided, deeply despairing, exultant, rooted in rich historical tradition and ethnic variety.

—JANN WENNER, founder of
Rolling Stone magazine, 1971

Rock 'n' roll is beautiful and it's ugly simultaneously. I mean, it's rock 'n' roll that brings people together in the mud in Woodstock. It's rock 'n' roll that starts black riots in Rochester and has cops beating people on the head for ten hours later. It's rock 'n' roll, you know. There's so many good things, so many bad things. It's so unpredictable.

—HOWARD STERN, radio talk show host

We mustn't be responsible, we must be *irresponsible*, artistically speaking. . . . Rock 'n' roll ought to be irresponsible.

—BONO, 1989

The end of World War II and the way the world changed in the wake of those cataclysms is what caused rock 'n' roll. It was human conflict and rebellion that created rock 'n' roll—not the other way around.

—DARYL HALL, of Hall & Oates, 1987

A lot of big bands in the States seem to be frighteningly ignorant of stuff that is really their own heritage. They have this rock and this heavy metal music in America that doesn't have any roots in rock 'n' roll and soul or anything. It's a creation of the 1970s. I'm talking about the Totos and the Rushes—those groups that sing, "We're a rock 'n' roll band!" or "We're rocking tonight!" And they don't have anything to do with rock 'n' roll, wouldn't know it if it bit them.

—ELVIS COSTELLO, 1983

Part of what we consider our fundamental rock 'n' roll heritage originated in Africa. Period. If you look back at any school of music or art, it steals ruthlessly from anything that excites it. That's a pretty normal process.

—PETER GABRIEL, 1986

Rock music was a completely new musical form. It hadn't been around for 10 years when we started doing it. . . . At the beginning you felt like you were one of the chosen few, one of the only ones in the whole world who would get to play with this new toy.

—MICK JAGGER, 1994

When Phil and I started out, everyone hated rock 'n' roll. The record companies didn't like it at all—felt it was unnecessary evil. And the press—interviewers were always older than us, and they always let you know they didn't like your music. . . . Then along came the '60s and everybody suddenly got real young, and if you were over thirty, they didn't trust you.

—DON EVERLY, of the Everly Brothers

When I was a kid, rock 'n' roll was totally disreputable. I wanted to play rock 'n' roll but I wanted it to be respectable. I thought, gee, it'd be nice if rock 'n' roll had the acceptability that jazz has, that kind of cerebral appreciation. I loved the music, but not the stigma attached to it.

—JERRY GARCIA (1942–1995),
of the Grateful Dead, 1991

I never considered myself part of rock 'n' roll. I didn't believe that I was among the forerunners of the music, and I've never given myself a lick of credit for either inventing it or having anything to do with its birth. Cats like Chuck Berry and Little Richard and Bo Diddley . . . did some spirited music, and it broke through some thick barriers . . . [but] my stuff was more adult, filled with more despair than anything you'd associate with rock 'n' roll.

—RAY CHARLES

When I started singing [rock 'n' roll], I sang it a long time before I presented it to the public because I was afraid they wouldn't like it. I never heard nobody do it, and I was scared.

—LITTLE RICHARD, 1990

But you know, rock 'n' roll, at one time, nobody even wanted to hear it. They said, "What is this?"
—MICHAEL JACKSON, 1989

Anyone who says rock 'n' roll is a passing fad or a flash-in-the-pan trend along the music road has rocks in the head, dad!

—ALAN FREED (1922–1965), one of the first
disc jockeys to play rock 'n' roll on the radio

[Rock 'n' roll] will be gone by June.
—*VARIETY*, 1955

There'll always be some arrogant little brat who wants to make noise with a guitar. Rock 'n' roll will never die.

—DAVE EDMUNDS, 1985

The thing they call rock 'n' roll, what used to be called rock 'n' roll—it got decadent. . . . Then it became self-conscious, which I think is the death of any moment. It became self-conscious, involuted and kind of incestuous. The energy is gone. There is no longer a belief.

—JIM MORRISON (1943–1971), 1969

Actually, rock 'n' roll is an asinine phrase. It was coined after the fact. White rock 'n' roll is really a combination of rhythm and blues and country—the new wave of country music.

—PHIL EVERLY, of the Everly Brothers

Well, I'm pretty sick of rock music, pretty sick of anything in that sphere. The thing is, I love playing it—I find it thrilling to make, but I know that once I make it I'm never going to listen to it again.   —BRIAN ENO, record producer

How can you be a rebel when rebellion is the norm? Rock 'n' roll has lost its staying power as a revolutionary force, it really has, and there's no way it can get it back.

—STING

Remember when you used to watch TV in the '60s and you'd see Perry Como in a cashmere sweater? That's what rock 'n' roll is becoming. It's your parents' music.

—NEIL YOUNG

Rock 'n' roll has become respectable. What a bummer.

—RAY DAVIES, of the Kinks

Rock 'n' roll is a bit like Las Vegas; guys dressed up in their sisters' clothes pretending to be rebellious and angry, but not really angry about anything. —STING

> Rock 'n' roll is not so much a question of electric guitars as it is striped pants. —DAVID LEE ROTH

It's all a consequence of making rock 'n' roll really important. America is the only country that thinks this way about rock 'n' roll. Everywhere else it's just pop music. Over here it's culture—because it's the only culture you've got. So you make it more important than it is. —ELVIS COSTELLO

You don't have to have the intelligence of a brain surgeon to play rock 'n' roll. —STING, 1983

Be-bop-a-lula, she's my baby. —PAUL SIMON, when asked what the smartest thing he ever heard anybody say in rock 'n' roll was

Rock 'n' roll is not supposed to be perfect.

—GLENN FREY, of the Eagles

Pop has become solemn, irrelevant, and boring. What it needs now is more noise, more size, more sex, more violence, more gimmickry, more vulgarity. Above all, it desperately needs a new messiah who will take things right back to the glamour, power, and insanity of the Elvis Presley age.

—PETE TOWNSHEND

There are those of us that are still dreaming, still trying to breathe life into the old forms of rock 'n' roll. Rock 'n' roll has given so much to me, and I want to give something back, but I don't want to be a part of what it's become, this ugly monster, this dinosaur.

—BONO, 1987

Rock 'n' roll has really been bringing me down lately. It's in great danger of becoming an immobile, sterile fascist that constantly spews its propaganda on every arm of the media. . . . It lets in lower elements and shadows that I don't think are necessary.

—DAVID BOWIE, 1976

Rock 'n' roll is the lowest form of life known to man.

—ELVIS COSTELLO

Rock 'n' roll is an asylum for emotional imbeciles.

—RICHARD NEVILLE,
of the Neville Brothers

Rock 'n' roll is ridiculous. It's absurd. In the past, U2 was trying to duck that. Now we're wrapping our arms around it and giving it a great big kiss. It's like I say onstage, "Some of this bullshit is pretty cool."

—BONO

Rock is very, very important and very, very ridiculous.

—PETE TOWNSHEND, 1994

Rock 'n' roll is a communicable disease.

—*The New York Times*, 1956

I don't give a fuck about rock 'n' roll.

—STING

It's no longer sex, drugs, and rock 'n' roll. It's crack, masturbation, and Madonna.

—SCOTT WEILAND, of Stone Temple Pilots

There is nothing conceptually better than rock 'n' roll. No group, be it Beatles, Dylan or Stones, have ever improved on "Whole Lot of Shaking," for my money. Or maybe I'm like our parents. That's my period, and I dig it, and I'll never leave it.

—JOHN LENNON (1940–1980)

The Rock 'n' Roll Hall of Fame was a great idea when it started out but I think they ought to close it. I think it's full.

—NEIL YOUNG

At the time the Rolling Stones started off in England, rock 'n' roll had degenerated to where it meant, like Fabian and Frankie Avalon. 'Cause by '59, who did you have left? Elvis was in the army. Buddy Holly had taken the dive. Jerry Lee Lewis was disgraced. Little Richard had thrown his bracelets and jewelry into the sea and gone back to church.

—KEITH RICHARDS, 1989

Rock has always been the devil's music. You can't convince me that it isn't.   —DAVID BOWIE, 1976

All of the rock music being aired today is demonically inspired. Any individual listening to it is entering into a communion with a wickedness and evil spawned in hell.

—JIMMY SWAGGERT, evangelist and Jerry
Lee Lewis's cousin

Rock 'n' roll is a means of pulling the white man down to the level of the Negro. Rock 'n' roll is part of a plot to undermine the morals of the youth of our nation. It is sexualistic, unmoralistic, and . . . brings people of both races together.

—North Alabama White Citizens Council,
circa 1950s

What is it about rock 'n' roll that so many people in the state and church fear? My personal opinion is that when you look at rock 'n' roll historically, no other art form on the face of the earth ever brought together a black man, a rich man, a Jew, and a Christian all under one roof. . . . I am convinced the more I learn about politics that there are a group of people in this country that fear anything that brings us together, because they hold the power over us by fear, and they want us to hate each other because we have different skin color or maybe don't go to the same church.

—BUTCH STONE, band manager and
anticensorship activist

[Rock 'n' roll is] just entertainment, and the kids who like to identify their youthful high spirits with a solid beat are thus possibly avoiding other pursuits that could be harmful to them.

—BILL HALEY

[Rock 'n' roll] is sung, and written for the most part by cretinous goons; and by means of its almost imbecilic reiterations and sly, lewd—in plain fact, dirty—lyrics it manages to be the martial music of every sideburned delinquent on the face of the earth. This rancid-smelling aphrodisiac I deplore.

—FRANK SINATRA, 1957

Sex, Love, & Marriage

chapter two

SLIPPERY
WHEN WET

**ex is power and sex leaves you power-less.** —AXL ROSE, of Guns N' Roses, 1992

Simone de Beauvoir in *The Second Sex* wrote about this thing called sexual valuation, meaning you are who you fuck. You cannot get back at a man that way, but a man can get back at a woman by sexually devaluating her. —COURTNEY LOVE, of Hole, 1995

There are men out there who think that women don't mind if they don't reach orgasm during sex. This philosophy probably dates back to the beginning of time and is hopelessly tangled in a bullshit moralistic-religious quagmire, where the man's orgasm was used for procreation and deemed okay with God and a woman's climax was the stuff of pure, decadent sin. For a woman to desire was a big no-no. For a woman to enjoy sex was unthinkable. —HENRY ROLLINS, 1995

I find it very difficult to draw a line between what's sex and what isn't. It can be very, very sexy to drive a car, and completely unsexy to flirt with someone at a bar. —BJÖRK, 1994

Everything that lives has to have sex. I mean, televisions don't have sex. Light bulbs don't. . . . If you regard the computer revolution as a living organism, it will also die and needs to have sex, so you may be confronted with the possibility of computers fucking in 50 years. I've got a feeling humanity is about to die out and replace itself with electronic babies. —ROBYN HITCHCOCK

Beyond sex is God. —MARVIN GAYE (1939–1984)

I'm not trying to sell sex. I just don't like wearing a lot of clothes onstage.

—SHEILA E.

Ultimately, I want to make everybody horny.

—PATTI SMITH

I think it's an asset to a performer to be sexually attractive.

—CARLY SIMON

If I was a girl, I'd rather fuck a rock star than a plumber.

—GENE SIMMONS, of Kiss

Having 100 girls isn't any different from one girl, except I like it a whole lot better. —TED NUGENT

I'm pro-heterosexual. I can't get enough of women. I have sex as often as possible. . . . It's really hard to maintain a one-on-one relationship if the other person is not going to allow me to be with other people. —AXL ROSE, of Guns N' Roses

I make love as often as I wash my hair.

—TERENCE TRENT D'ARBY, 1988

> **Sexual intercourse is a lovely t'ing.**
> —BOB MARLEY (1945–1981), 1975

Don't forget, the penis is mightier than the sword.

—SCREAMIN' JAY HAWKINS

Passions are dangerous. They cause you to lust after other men's wives. —MARVIN GAYE (1939–1984)

Sex is so much better [sober]! It's amazing! My wife is thrilled! She's like, "Oh, my God! This is the shit, man!"

—TOMMY LEE, of Mötley Crüe

My social life has been going like this: I go up to a girl and ask if she wants a drink. She says, "No." I say, "How about a dance?" She says, "No." And I say, "Then I suppose a fuck would be out of the question."

—ANDREW GOLD, guitar player for Linda Ronstadt, 1983

Do I enjoy having sex? Yes, I'd be crazy not to. I was deprived in high school, and I'm gonna make up for it now.

—BRET MICHAELS, of Poison

I was a little gigolo when I was 17. And I had older women picking me up when I was 15. So I've been around the block a time or two, you know?

—JON BON JOVI, 1995

I've gone through a whoring stage. That's fine, it's good to learn what it's like to be a whore.

—PERRY FARRELL, of Jane's Addiction

I don't believe in chastity. Sex is only corrupting if your attitude is that it's bad. I thought that, even when I was a little girl. I had a bad reputation even in junior high school because my skirts were too tight. . . . I had sex when I was 17.

—LINDA RONSTADT, 1983

Years ago, but that was simply because I was sent to a good school. There weren't any girls around, so you had to practice on men.

—ROBYN HITCHCOCK, when asked if he'd ever had any homosexual encounters

When I said I was bisexual in the mid-70s, I was the first major star apart from David Bowie to admit that. A lot of people still don't believe it—all the blind people in the world. But I feel very easy about my sexuality now. I thought everybody knew anyway.

—ELTON JOHN, 1995

But I wish I had more support in the gay community. The gay community complains about people not being very visible, and then when an artist does something which is political and visible they don't support him. . . . The gay community just isn't that supportive of its own. That's kind of weird to me, because people

19

complained that I wasn't more visible in the old days, and that I wasn't "out" enough. Well, how much more "out" could I be?

—BOY GEORGE, 1996

I'm not homosexual and I'm not heterosexual. I'm . . . sexual.

—MICHAEL STIPE, of R.E.M., 1995

But I'm sort of a fag. I've got the same tastes as fags. I like to suck. I go for the rough-trade boys. I'm a total drag-queen fag.

—COURTNEY LOVE, of Hole, 1995

I feel that most gay men are so much more in touch with a certain kind of sensitivity that heterosexual men aren't allowed to be in touch with—their feminine side. Straight men need to be emasculated. . . . Every straight guy should have a man's tongue in his mouth at least once.   —MADONNA

There's nothing like a good piece of ass to inspire rock 'n' roll.

—TED NUGENT

Why did I get into rock 'n' roll? I got into rock 'n' roll to get laid.

—TERENCE TRENT D'ARBY

People gave me this hell just because I said, "I don't see nothing wrong with a little bump and grind." I didn't say anything that doesn't happen everywhere in the world. You just have to face it. Everybody bumps and grinds once in a while.

—R. KELLY, defending his 1994 hit single
"Bump and Grind," 1995

love the one
you're with

i **just hope we're a nice old couple living off the coast of Ireland or something like that— looking at our scrapbook of madness.**

—JOHN LENNON (1940–1980), on the future with Yoko Ono, 1971

He was my husband. He was my lover. He was my friend. He was my partner. And he was an old soldier who fought with me.

—YOKO ONO, on John Lennon

I have a feeling that Yoko may not be the greatest influence on [John Lennon]. I mean, I don't know, but I have a feeling that he's a far greater talent than she is.

—PHIL SPECTOR, record producer, on Yoko Ono and John Lennon's relationship, 1969

A hundred years from now, it's Yoko Ono the world's going to remember, not John Lennon or the Beatles.

—CHARLOTTE MOORMAN, performance artist, 1989

He was so gorgeous . . . Kurt. I don't know how I got lucky that way.

—COURTNEY LOVE, of Hole, on her late husband, Kurt Cobain, 1995

He had every social disease. . . . He was infested, and so was his hair. He hadn't taken a bath for months. Or combed his hair. I think it was not so much rock 'n' roll, and not so much the road, as it [was] that nobody was taking care of him. You can always spot a bachelor!

—GAIL ZAPPA, on her late husband, Frank Zappa

The only time I ever punched Tina with my fist was the last fight we had. I hit her after she kneed me in the chest. Prior to that, our fights, or our little slaps, or whatever they were, were all just about attitude. . . . It was always because she was looking sad and wouldn't tell me what was wrong with her on the stage, and that would really depress me. So after the show, I'd end up slapping her or something. But then we'd be okay.

—IKE TURNER

I felt very loyal to Ike, and I didn't want to hurt him. I knew if I left him there'd be no one to sing, so I was caught up in guilt. I mean, sometimes, after he beat me up, I'd end up feeling very sorry for him. I'd be sitting there all bruised and torn and feeling sorry for him. I was just . . . brainwashed? Maybe I was brainwashed.

—TINA TURNER, on her abusive marriage to
Ike Turner, 1984

It looked in the press like it was all my fault that I attacked Sharon and that I should be locked up and horse-whipped. There's two sides to the coin. I mean, one doesn't exactly go home and just try to kill his fucking wife! I caught her lying concerning a party she was havin' whilst I was on tour . . . it's a long story. But this one morning I'd been on a booze and drug binge which basically left me going temporarily fucking nuts. The whole thing now seems like a bad dream, I remember going through the motions of trying to strangle her without thinking about it, almost watching myself put my hands around her neck. The next thing I was wrestling with two real policemen and being taken off and thrown into jail. I was certifiably insane at that point. I was temporarily totally mad.

—OZZY OSBOURNE, on his arrest for the
attempted murder of his first wife, 1995

Our needs are different; it seemed impossible to stay together. James needs a lot more space around him—aloneness, remoteness, more privacy. I need more closeness, more communication. He's more abstract in our relationship. I'm more concrete. He's more of a . . . poet, and I'm more of a . . . reporter.

—CARLY SIMON, on her troubled marriage to
James Taylor, 1981

I tried to mold her into what I thought I wanted. I realized too late that you just can't do that. You can't teach a person to be affectionate. By nature, she's a cold person. She's reserved. She's very disciplined. . . . So I tried to teach her to be warm and funny and loving and affectionate. She tried to do it, but you really can't teach someone to be what they aren't.

—ELVIS PRESLEY (1935–1977), on his wife,
Priscilla Presley

On top of the fact that I love the bitch to death, she keeps up with me, she keeps me going.

—KEITH RICHARDS, on his wife, Patti
Hansen, 1988

I love my wife more than anything in the world—I love being married. Marriage used to scare the shit out of me. Now it doesn't.

—SCOTT WEILAND, of Stone Temple Pilots

Another thing the press have said is that I'll probably calm down now that I'm married. Well, they haven't met my husband! When you meet someone, they don't tame you, they make you feel more content and just in love basically. People are always trying to get around the fact that I got married, because it isn't very rock 'n' roll, is it?

—KAT BJELLAND, of Babes in Toyland, 1994

I read in an article somewhere that in relationships, when you get beyond the initial sexual attraction, you realize that you sort of want to be like the other person. And I thought, "Yeah, I'd like to be like my wife." She's incredibly focused and intelligent, and she's cooler than anybody I know.   —JON BON JOVI, 1995

I want to be married again. I want to have more children. I have a great desire to be in that space where marriage takes you. That's the space where we're most relaxed and able to give and receive maximum love. . . . I used to think friction was needed to fire up a relationship. But forget friction, man, I want harmony.

—STEVIE WONDER, 1995

I feel lonely making love to my wife. It's like we're all here, but we're totally isolated; no matter how close you are to one person or a hundred, you're always totally isolated.

—STING

> **I got married for all the wrong reasons. I thought it would save me from all the misery I was going through.**
> —ELTON JOHN, 1995

I wasn't happy with marriage; I went into it wrong. I think I just find it hard to live with anybody. I'm a very solitary person, actually, kind of selfish that way. I like my own company. I like thinking on my own, I like writing on my own. I find it hard to be perpetually enthusiastic about somebody else's life all the time.

—DAVID BOWIE, 1983

I think I'm a fairly loyal person, too. Although there's probably a few girlfriends who would disagree with me.

—ROD STEWART, 1988

I'm one of those people who wanted to be married just once and for the rest of my life; one commitment, with one common goal.

—BILLY JOEL, 1982

Being able to give yourself to another person is the bravest thing in the world and it's the bravest thing I ever do.

—TANYA DONELLY, of Belly

Maybe I'll find someone who will just stay at home and rub my feet at night. That's the kind of man I'm lookin' for myself. But, uh, I'll take what I can get. —CHRISSIE HYNDE, of the Pretenders, 1980

People often ask me what I look for in women. I look for ME in women! —GENE SIMMONS, of Kiss

By chance, most of the men I've fallen in love with have turned out to be helpful to my career.

—MADONNA

What I learned is that when you fall in love, you've lost contact with reality. You are slowly giving the power of your will and mind to something else. That's where possessiveness, jealousy comes from. Out of all the emotions we get, jealousy is the worst of the negatives. —BARRY WHITE

But I think the things that bring us to grief are plain to see: jealousy, lack of faith, lack of trust. I'm not a great believer that there are deeper secrets behind the distance between [men and women] that are locked up somewhere waiting to be discovered. Generally, I don't think people talk very much, regardless of who they are. They might say more words these days, but whether they're talking to each other is another matter.

—ELVIS COSTELLO, speculating on the source
of conflict between the sexes, 1983

For an intimate relationship with one's mate, the only really important thing is feelings. That's the main thing: whether or not someone's right or wrong doesn't make a damned bit of difference! You can be seething about something that's so petty you hardly dare bring it up, but the fact is that you must say, "I am furious."

—JAMES TAYLOR, 1981

We go through life thinking we can give love and receive love on our own terms, and then one day we wake up to realize that we can't have love on any terms at all.

—DON HENLEY, 1990

You want some romance, some sweetness, you scrape together some change for a quart of chow mein. And a pint of Thunderbird or maybe somethin' weird like cactus wine. You and the lady finish it all up. Got to be chow mein or the magic don't work. Lean the lady up on one of them big Pontiacs—we in the fifties now—be sweet, and she slide right down the tailfin and into your arms. Lord bless and keep them automotive engineers. Gave a country boy a reason to sing in that dirty old city. —WILSON PICKETT

[Physical] pleasure is linked to eternal love, a love beyond this world. Sure it starts with the body, and that's great. That's wonderful. It starts with just one kiss. But a really heavy union between two lovers can be a link to God just as surely as a monk praying in a monastery.

—STEVIE WONDER, 1995

Love is like a longing, and energy. It's like magnetism, it's like gravity. And at its highest it's about spiritual salvation.

—PETE TOWNSHEND, 1989

You are attracted to men who have material things because that's what pays the rent and buys you furs. That's the security. That lasts longer than emotion.

—MADONNA, 1985

The way that people in America talk about love is totally incorrect. The American idea of love is ridiculous. It's a fantasy, a fairy-tale. It's based on goals that cannot be achieved and fantasies that don't exist.

—FRANK ZAPPA (1940–1993)

I think the whole conception of love is something that the previous generation invents to justify their having created you. You know I think the real reason children are born is because parents are so bored . . . they have children to amuse themselves. . . . Then, to justify to the kid the reason he exists they tell him there is such a thing as love and that's where you come from.

—RICHARD HELL, of Television, 1976

Romance can only exist if your love is imperiled.

—ROBYN HITCHCOCK, 1995

Love.

—a young GEORGE HARRISON'S response when asked what he considered the most important thing in life

When I write love songs, people think they're really soppy—but I see love as a consolation for the boredom of life.

—MARTIN GORE, of Depeche Mode

I deal with the subject of love from the viewpoint of someone who [hasn't] experienced it.   —IGGY POP

But, you know, I don't think I've ever written a love song. No, I don't think I have. I wouldn't quite know how to go about it. I've written cynical songs about love. But no, I've never written a proper love song. I mean, this is much to the regret of all the women in my life.

—PETE TOWNSHEND, 1989

I mean, I never went to a dance [in high school], never went out on a date, I never went steady. It became pretty awful for me. Except, of course, I could go see bands, and that was the kick. . . . So I was in love a lot of the time, but mostly with guys in bands that I had met. For me, knowing that Brian Jones was out there, and later that Iggy Pop was out there, made it kind of hard for me to get interested in the guys around me. I had, uh, bigger things in mind.

—CHRISSIE HYNDE, of the Pretenders, 1980

A long time ago I used to get drunk and hang out a lot around mental institutions, because the girls there are all loose and they are . . . fun, you know? So I kind of fell in love with this girl, and every week they took her upstairs to the fifth floor to have shock treatments. They would strap her into a wheelchair. Before they took her up she was fine. Then she came down, and she was like a zombie and didn't even know who I was.

—JOEY RAMONE, of the Ramones, 1979

Motown, Rhythm & Blues, and Rap

sweet soul music

 combination of rats, roaches, love, and guts.

—BERRY GORDY, founder of Motown, defining his record label's sound

[It's] something that you would have to say on paper was impossible. They took black music and beamed it directly to the white American teenager.

—JERRY WEXLER, V.P. of Atlantic Records, on Motown's greatest achievement

They call me Lady Soul, so let me tell you something about soul. Soul is something creative, something active. Soul is honesty. I sing to people about what matters. I sing to the realists; people who accept it like it is. I express problems. There are tears when it's sad and smiles when it's happy. It seems simple to me, but to some, feelings take courage.

—ARETHA FRANKLIN

Soul is the way black folks sing when they leave themselves alone.

—RAY CHARLES

Soul is not about black or white music. Soul is a physical manifestation of higher consciousness. It's a going from the right lobe straight out to the world, using the physical body as a springboard for an insight. . . . Soul is a howling at the moon—and having the moon respond.

—DARYL HALL, of Hall & Oates, 1987

[Soul singers] were very real and able to lay it down and sing songs about really intimate struggles and be somehow lifted up by singing about them. . . . It's the basic reason that people do music in the first place I guess.

—JOAN OSBORNE, 1995

Funk is the soul going deep into itself. It's getting to that place which is the lost part of your soul. . . . Sure it's a groove thing, and it's a nasty thing. It's playing between the beats. It's got the complexity of jazz and the earthiness of the blues, but it's even more complicated than that. It's got those syncopated complications that make you wanna move. —STEVIE WONDER, 1976

Soul music . . . elevates "feeling" above all else. . . . Soul music assumes a shared experience, a relationship with the listener, as in blues, where the singer confirms and works out the feelings of the audience. In this sense it remains sacramental.

—CLIVE ANDERSON, British author

Soul to me is a feeling, a lot of depth and being able to bring to the surface that which is happening inside, to make the picture clear. The song doesn't matter. . . . It's just the emotion, the way it affects other people. —ARETHA FRANKLIN

Now I'd been singing spirituals since I was three, and I'd been hearing the blues for just as long. So what could be more natural than to combine them? It didn't take any thinking, didn't take any calculating. All the sounds were there, right at the top of my head. . . . I got a lot of flak because some people felt it was like an abomination of the church, but then people began to realize, "No, that ain't it at all, the man is just singing what he feels. He's got to sing what's in him." —RAY CHARLES

I think British soul tends to be less conventional. American soul music seems to be going through a phase right now where most of the songs are quite similar. They've found a formula that works, and I don't know if they've exhausted it, but they're employing it quite a bit. —DES'REE, 1995

The people who I was really trying to emulate, especially in the beginning, were the soul singers and R&B singers who had that ability to be very real, be very human, be vulnerable and maybe foolish, but at the same time very strong and very sexy.

—JOAN OSBORNE, 1995

Otis is the only one I can think of now who [sings soul] best. He gets over to the people what he's talking about, and he does it in so few words that if you read them on paper they might not make any sense. But when you hear the way he sings them, you know exactly what he is talking about. —STEVE CROPPER, Otis Redding's guitar
player and occasional collaborator

Sam and Dave were really underrated over here [in England]. Over here it's all Marvin Gaye and that sort of smooth soul. Sam and Dave were rough, and it's their roughness I love.

—DAVE STEWART, of Eurythmics, 1983

he blues had a baby, and they called it rock 'n' roll. —MUDDY WATERS (1915–1983)

Before Muddy [Waters] died, he told me, "Don't let the blues die." We as blues players don't have the recognition that I hope we could get. But who am I? I can't do nothing about it. All we can do is just play. —BUDDY GUY, 1989

Look at the blues! I mean, you keep having to go back to that. In our music, rock 'n' roll, the blues are our mentor, our godfather, everything. We'll never lose that, however diversified and modernistic and cliché-ridden with synthesizers it becomes. We'll never, ever be able to renounce the initial heritage.

—DAVID BOWIE, 1983

There ain't no blues revival goin' on. The music has always been there. Never really gone anywhere. The same cats have been making the same great music all along. What is different now is there's a chance for the music to be listened to by a lot of people again. And that, let me tell you, is good news for everyone.

—STEVIE RAY VAUGHN (1954–1990)

Blues music been around ever since America been around, but nobody has given it its just dues. The world has seemed to be able to keep black history from America. This is where the damage is being done to the blues. It's great to be able to get any part of our thing over at any time, because this history of ours has never been taught. Nowhere.

—WILLIE DIXON (1915–1992), 1989

If you want to learn to play anything you want to play and learn how to make songs yourself, you take your guitar and you go to where a crossroads is. A big black man will walk up there at the stroke of midnight and take your guitar and tune it.

—LADELL JOHNSON, dates unknown, repeating what his brother, legendary bluesman Tommy Johnson, told him; like Robert Johnson (no relation), Tommy was reported to have sold his soul to the devil in exchange for the ability to play the blues

Those men who raised blues-singing to professional status tended to be social outcasts, whether through temperamental malaise like Robert Johnson, or through physical affliction (usually blindness) like Blind Lemon Jefferson. They had no home, but wandered from city to city, seeking a livelihood from song.

—WILFRID MELLERS, *Music in a New Found Land*

[While sleeping at a train station in Mississippi in 1903, I was awakened by] the weirdest music I ever heard. [A] lean, loose-jointed Negro had commenced plunking a guitar beside me while I slept. His clothes were rags; his feet peeped out of his shoes. As he played, he pressed a knife on the strings of the guitar in a manner popularized by Hawaiian guitarists who used steel bars. The effect was unforgettable. —W. C. HANDY (1873–1958), often called the father of the blues, recalling the first time he heard the sound that inspired him to create his style of music

The things people used to say about those I thought of as the greats in the business, the blues singers, used to hurt me. They spoke of them as illiterate and dirty. The blues had made me a better living than any I had, so this was when I really put my fight on. A few whites gave me the blah-blah about the blues singers, but mostly it was Negro people, and that's why it hurt.

—B. B. KING, 1966

Rhythm & Blues was looked down on. It was low-class music, it was wild music, it was sexual music, it was "dirty" music. So as far as we were concerned, it was the most glamorous life in the world.

—JULIAN BOND, former leader of the Student National Coordinating Committee, a minorities' rights group

My eyes swept the [dance] floor anxiously, then suddenly I saw the lightning strike. The dancers seemed electrified. Something within them came suddenly to life. An instinct that wanted so much to live, to fling its arms and to spread joy, took them by the heels.

—W. C. HANDY (1873–1958), on the first
time he played "St. Louis Blues" at a club
in 1914

When you're playing and all of a sudden you realize your toes . . . are . . . tighten[ing] up, and you get a chill all the way up your back because of what you just gave somebody and they gave it back. That's probably the biggest thrill. Or, you're playing someplace and you hit a note and people start screaming—that's it. You gave them a thrill, or you soothed them. That's what the blues do to me.

—STEVIE RAY VAUGHN (1954–1990), on
the greatest part about playing the blues

Now that Stevie is gone, the blues world feels a little different. Like the rest of us Stevie believed there was something special about playing the blues, something worth spending a lifetime on. Stevie was a great talent who also understood what keeps the music alive through the years. I've said that playing the blues is like having to be black twice. Stevie missed on both counts, but I never noticed.

—B. B. KING, on Stevie Ray Vaughn, 1993

Stevie did so much for the blues. I keep saying that he had a skeleton key and opened up the warehouse and let us all out, because our music was locked in the back room. It wasn't on the radio, it wasn't on the television. Stevie did open those doors when he came out and started playing his guitar like he did. He exploded and helped us all. —BUDDY GUY, on Stevie Ray Vaughn, 1993

That's what I started to appreciate about a lot of the blues. These guys were really telling stories, and it wasn't so important if the music was perfect. What mattered was, they grabbed you with their convictions. —ROBERT CRAY

When the blues singer sits there and pours out his heart, he's purging his soul a little bit, and he's doing so for all the audience, so [they] can sympathize and maybe get a little emotion out, too. I know that when I can get emotion out, I suddenly feel more alive, just as if I was pulsing with new blood in a way I simply don't when I try to suppress things. —PETER GABRIEL, 1986

Sounds like the blues are composed of feeling, finesse, and fear.
—BILLY GIBBONS, of ZZ Top

An autobiographical chronicle of catastrophe, expressed lyrically.
—RALPH ELLISON (1914–1994),
author, his definition of the blues

I don't want to change nothing about R&B. I just want to make my mark. I sing from the heart, about how I really feel, not about killing my brother or sticking him up. I sing about the hard times black people go through, how we need to strive to make them better and bring on some hope. —L. V., 1996

> **Blues is just a feel of what's goin' on, whether you're an old black man in Mississippi or a white kid in Philly.**
> —G. LOVE, of G. Love and Special Sauce, 1995

I remember one time a guy asked me, "Hey, man, do you think a white cat could ever sing the blues?" Which is a legitimate question. It didn't hurt my feelings. I feel that anybody, if you ever have the blues bad enough, with the background that dictates to the horror and suffering of the blues, I don't give a damn if he's green, purple—he can git to ya. —RAY CHARLES

I'd never even imagined that white guys could sing the blues authentically—let alone white women.
—BONNIE RAITT, 1994

Nothing. —ERIC CLAPTON'S response when asked what
he owes black musicians

Well, we're all in the same boat.
—his response when asked why not, 1982

American blues, to me, just means a mix of various African sounds. It's not American music, it's African music directly imported from Africa.

—ALI FARKA TOURÉ, native of Mali and
master of the one-string gurkel

I love blues, and I love the straightforwardness of the country lyric. And you can be sneaky with both, which I enjoy.

—LYLE LOVETT, 1992

The blues is a chair, not a design for a chair . . . it is the first chair. It is a chair for sitting on, not chairs for looking at or being appreciated. You sit on that music. . . . We didn't sound like anybody else, that's all. I mean we didn't sound like the black musicians because we weren't black. And because we were brought up on a different kind of music and atmosphere, and so "Please Please Me" and "From Me to You" and all those were our version of the chair. We were building our own chairs.

—JOHN LENNON (1940–1980), 1970

fight the power

I love rap. I learn from rap. . . . I believe that rappers are the *griots*, the African storytellers in the village. They're verbal historians telling stories that are clear and real and need to be heard. Listen hard and you'll hear the pain. Without feeling that pain yourself, you'll never understand. And what we don't understand, we can't change, can't heal. I hate it when the very folks who should be listening to rap are attacking it so hard they miss the point. The point is that the children and the neighborhoods—the whole country, man—is drowning in violence.   —STEVIE WONDER, 1995

It's pretty easy to draw parallels between the war being waged now against rap and the kind of resistance that greeted the early rock and rollers of the '50s. To paraphrase Pete Townshend, it's not for us to judge the music that's being made in the streets; we just have to get out of the way.

—VERNON REID, of Living Colour

This is our voice. If it wasn't for rap, you would never know that these horrors are going on in the community.

—VINNIE BROWN,
of Naughty by Nature, 1995

Rap is the CNN of young black America.

—CHUCK D

I think rap [is] America's punk.

—MICK JONES, of the Clash

[Rappers] do more for our communities than basketball or football players. We don't ever leave our communities.

—LUTHER CAMPBELL, of 2 Live Crew, 1995

We don't come off on the gang-banging tip, we come off as kids from around the way. The delivery makes us different; that's where the comedy comes from. When you preach to people, they don't want to hear it. But if you talk shit, like "Yo, this guy tried to jack somebody and got his ass killed in the process," it works better. We show 'em the dark side in hopes that they walk away from it.

—B-REAL, of Cypress Hill, 1992

We know how much drugs, guns, and nonsense are in the street because that's where we come from. But there are so many different aspects to urban life and that's what we put on our records. Our minds might be in the gutter at times, but what do we do for fun? We don't shoot. We don't rob people anymore. We party. So that's what we put into our music.

—KAY GEE, of Naughty by Nature, 1995

I have no messages because I've learned that sometimes people don't take too kindly to rappers preaching to them, so I gave people what they want: fat-ass beats, fat-ass lyrics, and no substance at all.

—MC LYTE

I use a microphone like a plumber uses a tool.
—SCHOOLY D

We don't glorify this lifestyle [in gangsta rap]. We're glorifying our people—the negative and the positive. Our message is be real and don't let nobody oppress you.   —HAVOC, of Mobb Deep, 1995

The media created the buzz of rap being so terrible, but terrible is the ghetto shit we write about. We put it in their faces. Mother-fuckers losing their lives. The fucked-up system. They don't want to hear about it.   —SNOOP DOGGY DOGG, 1995

Demonstrate your gift, not your breast . . . not what is between your legs. . . . The American people have an appetite like a swine, and you are feeding the swine with the filth of degenerate culture.

—LOUIS FARRAKHAN, religious leader
of the Islam Nation, addressing rappers
at the Million Man March on
Washington, D.C., 1995

There was a time when people at the bottom of society listened to the blues, which had some anger in it, some raunchy humor and some bad-man characters . . . but it also had a lot else. Everything was always presented in balance, as part of a more complete picture of human life. Gangsta rap takes the worst out there and just wallows in it.   —MARTHA BAYLES, music scholar and
author of *Hole in Our Soul*, 1995

[Gangsta rap] is drama. If they weren't just venting that on records, they might be doing it. Because they're just representing what they see every day and making it theatrical. Do you think Ice-T ever killed a cop? It's a world you don't understand, anyway. It scares you, it terrifies you, sure.   —QUINCY JONES, record producer, 1995

I hate the term gangsta rap, but I don't feel confined by my image. I know where the fence is—where the boundaries of the image are—and I tend to get up real close to the fence and push on it and push on it and push on it. That's my nature.

—ICE CUBE, 1993

I'm trying to get rid of that jacket that's been put on my back—that I'm a gangsta rapper. That's not my thing. My thing is to be true to myself and try to educate and entertain kids. I have children of my own, and I realize that other people have children, too. I also realize that they don't know any more what the fuck to do with their children than I do. —COOLIO, 1995

I understand that some of the younger kids can't take the harsher words, so sometimes I'm torn whether to put out clean versions [of my songs] so they can get the message of my music too, or whether I should keep it the way it is. But the harsh language has always been around and will continue. If all rappers stop cursing, you think everyone will stop using those words?
—SCHOOLY D, 1993

Explain to [your children] that because I'm talking about [sex and violence and street life] doesn't mean that it's okay. This comes from someone who just spent 11 and a half months in a maximum-security jail, got shot five times, and was wrongly convicted of a crime he didn't commit. This is not from a normal person.
—TUPAC SHAKUR (1971–1996), on what parents should tell their kids before allowing them to listen to a Shakur album, 1996

I think if it wasn't for rap, I'd be in jail or something. I think I'd a murdered something. —TRAGEDY

My drive to create is really to help my friends. I'm not driven like some artists who say they have to make this stuff; I'm really driven by the results. Rap is nothing hard for me to do because it's my life—it's easy. —ICE-T, 1992

It seems that if you're black and you rhyme, you rap. I consider myself a poet. If you get labeled as just a rapper . . . you get held back. . . . Being just an MC is quite a narrow minded view, y'know?
—TRICKY, 1995

There's no such thing as rap music. Rap is a rhyming lyrical form over any kind of music. So long as there's different types of music, rap will always be around. Besides, there will always be people that can't sing. —FRESH PRINCE

If people paid closer attention in English class when they were talking about literature, if they knew what a good poem or a good short story was, they'd know what a good rap song was.

—MISTA LAWRENCE, of Black Sheep

Real rap comes from the soul and the mind, from the inner self.

—CHUCK D

Rap's a very fashionable music to like. I'd say rap's like starlight to me. By the time it reaches you, it ain't there anymore. It's removed from the neighborhood that it's intended for. I think that when it's really true, it's for, like, a two-block neighborhood somewhere that we don't live in. And all we can do is admire it at a distance.

—ELVIS COSTELLO

Rap wasn't made for Middle America. But that's not necessarily saying you have to be from the ghetto or the city to understand it. If you're focused and you have enough awareness of yourself and you have enough interest in different cultures and also in words and music, it's open to everybody.

—PETE NICE

Rap is like the polio vaccine. At first no one believed in it. Then once they knew it worked, everyone wanted it.

—GRANDMASTER FLASH

Rap's taking over the world. Literally. I don't mean just bumping all other music out of the box. But taking over to the point where everybody in the fucking world, from kids to grownups, will like rap.

—TIM DOG

Rap is teaching white kids what it means to be black, and that causes a problem for the infrastructure.

—CHUCK D

The '80s are best forgotten because the decade was just so repetitive. A lot of bad things were born out of sort of stealing from the old days. Rap music is one of the best things about the '80s.

—JOHNNY MARR, of the Smiths, 1989

I love that hip-hop has become international. I love it when I go to France and hear French *hip-hooop* groups. I love when I go to England and hear British hip-hop groups. I love to go see hip-hop groups all through Africa. Hip-hop has taken a lot of brothers and sisters who might be doing negative things and have gotten into the rap world to see other people's way of life.

—AFRIKA BAMBAATAA

What I liked about rap—that sense of community with people trying to make the best records, for either artistic or competitive reasons—[is that it] became a way to make money. When I started, nobody had really made money doing it, so that wasn't the goal. As it got bigger, it got less interesting. The new stuff began to sound like people capitalizing on what someone else had done. The intentions seemed wrong.

—RICK RUBIN, record producer who produced several Public Enemy albums at Def Jam, 1995

The best thing about being a famous rapper is going on stage and saying the same thing night after night and getting paid $8,000, $10,000, or $5,000 each time. And it's so fuckin' easy. My royalty checks alone will make you break your face smiling.

—TOO SHORT

The only thing that is makin' it really difficult for rap music right now is the fact that you can make a video and have a bullshit song come across as good. If there wasn't videos and video shows, there would be a lot of out-of-work motherfuckers, and maybe me too.

—L. L. COOL J

Rebels, Politics, and Punk

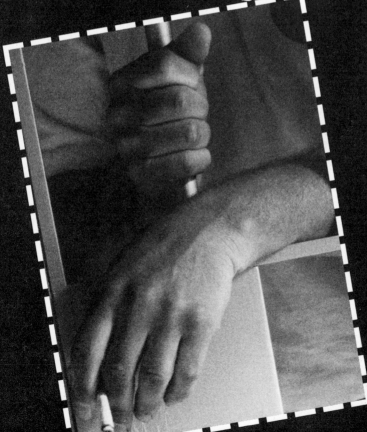

talkin' bout a revolution

think politics is an instrument of the devil. —BOB DYLAN

I think I'm a natural-born leader because I'm a good soldier. I know how to bow down to authority if it's authority that I respect. If Colin Powell was president, I'd follow him. I wanna get into politics. That's the way for us to overcome a lot of our obstacles. Nothing can stop power or recognize power but power.

—TUPAC SHAKUR (1971–1996), 1996

You can't trust politicians. It doesn't matter who makes a political speech. It's all lies . . . and it applies to any rock star who wants to make a political speech as well.

—BOB GELDOF, who was nominated for the Nobel Peace Prize in 1985

Politicians are necessary, and it'd be foolish to blame them for our troubles. They're just doing what they've always done—looking to survive, looking to climb, trying to please everyone at once, and grinning and lying while they're doing it.

—RAY CHARLES

I think if a lot of younger people would get into politics, some people with more '90s ideas, maybe the next decade we could see one cool person in there.   —ICE-T

It seems like . . . every presidential speech has an MTV background to it.   —JON BON JOVI, 1989

I made it clear from day one that he just had to forget it. I couldn't bear gettin' involved that way with any politician, least of all Reagan, and corrupt what is essentially a basic, humble dream of contentment he can't even understand.

—JOHN MELLENCAMP, his reaction upon learning that Ronald Reagan wanted to use "Pink Houses" as his presidential campaign song, 1987

We were trying to think of all these things we could do to him. For instance, in a show situation Tanya [Donelly] can pretty much vomit at will, so we were thinking of something with vomit.

—TOM GORMAN, of Belly, on sharing their *Tonight Show* appearance with Rush Limbaugh, 1995

I think it's a really mean deal that [Led Zeppelin] haven't been invited to the White House. Perhaps Jerry [Ford] thought we'd wreck the joint. —ROBERT PLANT, 1975

I wouldn't do anything with the Royal family. They're scum. Why do we subsidize this family of buffoons?

—ELVIS COSTELLO

The only thing that could possibly save British politics would be Margaret Thatcher's assassin. —MORRISSEY, on Margaret Thatcher, former British Prime Minister, who was defeated by John Major in 1992

Maybe I should be prime minister of England. I wouldn't mind being the first English president of the United States either. I'm certainly right wing enough.

—DAVID BOWIE, 1976

I met Bill Clinton. And I do think my aspirations are fucking higher than his, man. —DAVE PIRNER, of Soul Asylum, 1995

Nixon: You dress pretty wild, don't you?
Elvis Presley: Mr. President, you got your show to run and I got mine! —portion of the exchange between then President of the United States and the King of Rock 'n' Roll during their historic meeting

I don't know much about Watergate. It was terrible, wasn't it? I guess it was. Have you met Nixon? Is he happy? I saw him on TV last year, and he looked so unhappy!

—MICHAEL JACKSON, 1977

I been friends with Presidents! Johnson, Kennedy, Mr. President Habib Bourguida of Tunisia—you know where that is? I'm trying to get the dignitaries to send me over to Moscow to get the static outta the Hot Line and start everybody talking about love.

—JAMES BROWN, 1986

To talk about politics now is to talk about things that are incredibly personal things, like "What is a family? Who's Dad?" And this has a ripple effect in terms of social welfare and justice. We live in a very interesting moment. It feels like we're going backwards in some ways.

—LAURIE ANDERSON

I don't see a subject called politics, it's just right and wrong and what happens in life, what you're moved to write about. . . . There will always be clear headed people to argue the moral case. There will be bishops to argue against hanging and bishops to argue for hanging. But there should be songs to sing, as well. It's not like it's going to change a damn thing, but it gets it out of your head to say it. It stops you from kicking in the TV and maybe it does the same for somebody else. —ELVIS COSTELLO, 1989

I enjoy looking like a tart and thinking like a politician.

—P. J. HARVEY, 1995

That I'm political and serious. I'm actually a big goof. It's just people always bring [my sexual preference] up, and I answer, then that's what ends up in the article. But it's not like that's what I talk about all day at home. Somewhere between k. d. lang, lesbian—vegetarian lesbian—my music sieves between the cracks and ends up swimming at the bottom. —K. D. LANG, when asked what the biggest misconceptions about her are, 1995

Who wants politics in music? I find politics the single most uninspiring, unemotional, insensitive activity on this planet.

—ADAM ANT

I think it's reprehensible to take your music and put it in the service of a political party or some sort of cause. Because ultimately, music is worth more than any cause or party.

—FRANK ZAPPA (1940–1993), 1979

People think if you're a musician, you have to change the world. You're expected to be a politician, a guru—and a funky bass player.

—ME'SHELL NDEGEOCELLO, 1997

I think you have to make a distinction, not between art and politics, but between art and propaganda. Politics is a part of life, and you would be ignoring a whole aspect of life by leaving it out of songs.

—BRUCE COCKBURN

When you're as rich as I am, you don't have to be political.

—STING

We have to accept the reality that the musician is no longer a social force.

—BILL GRAHAM (1931–1990),
concert promoter

Music can't change the world.
—BOB GELDOF, organizer of the Live Aid concert in 1985, to benefit people starving in Ethiopia

Live Aid makes us feel a bit more comfortable to slightly relieve the discomfort of a nation in famine. But really the only way we can make them much more comfortable is by enduring a much higher level of discomfort ourselves. And we're not willing to do that. I'm not willing to do that. And I think that is evil.

—PETE TOWNSHEND

I don't know fuck about the U.N. I'd rather sing about rock 'n' roll and chicks. —TOM PETTY

I think you've got to be an idiot to think that any of that meant anything. It changes nothing. It does not make you a better person just because you've got a Pistols album. It doesn't lower your fuck-ing rent. It does nothing. It's escapism. All music is.

—JOHNNY ROTTEN, on the Sex Pistols'
revolutionary accomplishments, 1980

I don't pretend to give a message of any kind, except enjoy yourself and get laid. —LEMMY, of Motörhead

I could go on stage, unzip my pants, and hang my dick out and people would think it was some statement or something.

—BONO

The system want pure love songs like ol' Frank Sinatra, they don't want not'ing wit' no protest. It makes too much trouble.

—BOB MARLEY (1945–1981), 1975

I don't really think there's anything constructive about marching on the houses of Parliament or, you know, breaking down the walls of Babylon. I think we're more in favor of free enterprise. Bands like the Jam and the Clash seem to encourage these sorts of tribal move-ments, this gang mentality, and I don't like it.

—JOHN TAYLOR, of Duran Duran

People have come to us and said, "Do you realize how much power you have now? You could change the world with some of the things you say." And I say to them, "Leave me alone." Power is fleeting; so is ego. . . . Politicians have no idea how to save the world, so why should pop stars? —BARRY GIBB, of the Bee Gees, 1979

To expect music to be at the vanguard of any profound cultural change is asking too much of it. The real power of rock is more of a one-on-one kind of thing between the artist and the listener. I mean, despite the rise of arena rock, no one has ever tried to mobilize a stadium full of rock fans into a political force. Rock's association with the social movements of the '60s is greatly exaggerated, as well: let's not forget that Pete Townshend threw Abbie Hoffman off the stage at Woodstock. —ROBERT PALMER, rock critic and journalist, 1995

People who don't think that "entertainers" should have a voice in politics would just as soon leave war to the generals and politics to the "professional" politicians. To me, that's the opposite of a democracy. —JACKSON BROWNE

I believe in [our] ability to bridge the gap between entertainment and activism. —ZACH DE LA ROCHA, of Rage Against the Machine

There are no more political statements. The only thing rock fans have in common is their music.

—BOB PITTMAN, V.P. of MTV

If you're writing songs, there are two things that you just don't write about: politics and religion. We write about both.

—BONO

Who wants to save the bloody world?

—SIMON LE BON, of Duran Duran

I assume that we will blow ourselves up. I don't think people are gonna smart up in time. But on the other hand, I don't deny the possibility of hope. Action is the antidote to despair.

—JOAN BAEZ, 1983

We have a responsibility to humanity to keep the peace, to let the politicians know that nuclear war is not what God intended us to do.

—JAMES BROWN

Peace is a fictional word to me. —ICE CUBE, 1989

Being spokesman for a generation is the worst job I ever had.

—BILLY BRAGG

I'm not in a position to be seen as a spokesman of the generation. I mean, how can you be a spokesman of a generation if you've nothing to say, other than "Help!" —BONO

I'm learning how to listen to people instead of preaching at them. —JOAN BAEZ, 1976

I don't want to get up on a soapbox. It's not my desire to confess, and there aren't any burning social issues that I feel I have an exclusive handle on. —STING

I predict that if we don't listen, people are going to move to bloodshed. I know from listening to people in the street, if they do not see justice, then they are going to move.

—ICE-T

I guess I have a kind of war thing in me, but is better to die fighting for yar freedom than to be a prisoner all the days of your life.

—BOB MARLEY (1945–1981), 1975

The alternative [to violence] is for people to vent their frustrations through music. —MICK JONES, of the Clash, 1976

I'm still equally as pissed off about the things that made me pissed off a few years ago. It's people doing evil things to other people for no reason. And I just want to beat the shit out of them. That's the bottom line. And all I can do is scream into a microphone instead.

—KURT COBAIN (1967–1994), of
Nirvana, 1993

In 1994 Kurt Cobain died and Newt Gingrich came to power.

—KRIST NOVOSELIC, of Nirvana, 1995

Right now, with the Congress being swung to the right, my generation is in a lot of trouble. We have a lot of people making decisions for us who couldn't care less about us. So it's even more important that we get out there and fight. If we don't make the connection between voting and the problems that we have in our society and how one can change the other, then we're not going to succeed. We need to empower my generation.

—QUEEN LATIFAH, 1995

People need a leader. People need a leader more than a leader needs people.

—BOB DYLAN, 1984

Anarchy is the only slight glimmer of hope. Anybody should be able to go where he likes and do what he likes.

—MICK JAGGER

Shaving your head does not mean you're a rebel. The mythology of "live-fast-and-die-young" sickens me. I just want to throw up on those bastards.

—BONO

The government has a check-and-balance game: do wrong, consequences; do wrong, consequences. . . . The people cannot issue a consequence against the government. When they do wrong, what do we do?

—ICE-T, 1992

We're in this terrible morass of people absolutely not giving a shit about anybody but themselves. And a mean-spirited government that is essentially attacking people that can't defend themselves. That's the weakest people—the kids, the sick, the elderly. And I think we should fight back.

—LOU REED, 1989

But in truth there are only three types of people in the world: people who work, people who are not allowed to, and people who don't have to.

—ELVIS COSTELLO, 1983

To my mind America is the most racist, sexist, homophobic, violent society in the so-called free world.

—TERENCE TRENT D'ARBY

The one dilemma of living [in the United States] is giving so much money to a government I disapprove of. Every year there's another Cruise missile with my name on it.

—GEORGE MICHAEL

The thing I found incredible about Los Angeles was the flagrant inequality. You'd be on the Sunset Strip with people dangerously close to attacking you for money while all these Rolls-Royces were going by. —EXENE CERVENKA, of X

All around the Capitol it's blacks and ghettos, and we used to hear politicians sayin' this and that about how they'd help us. Then they'd put their blinders on and commute home to the suburbs. That's why we decided to tell it like it was.

—DR. KNOW, of Bad Brains; the group comes from the low-income area outside of Washington, D.C., 1995

If you stand up and say, well, I'm an American, that means you've got some kind of responsibility to America. Sometimes it seems like people going hungry is something that just happens a long ways away. But it happens here every day . . . in your hometown.

—BRUCE SPRINGSTEEN

Class is a depressing element of [English] society, and I don't think it has any positive aspects except that it gives you something to kick against. —ELVIS COSTELLO, 1983

Greed's so pervasive in this society. . . . It's every man for himself. It's about "Me, me, me, and damn the rest of the nation."

—DON HENLEY, 1990

So many young people seem to be getting quite pro-military these days. Somebody should remind them that they'll get their legs blown off if they go to war. —PAUL McCARTNEY

I tell you, history is, in part, a series of madmen deluding people into parting with their children for loathsome and tragic schemes.

—STING, 1985

I don't think the enemy is going to conquer America with atom bombs or missiles. I think they are just going to buy America or steal America and sell it back to them.

—BOB DYLAN, 1983

I just found it rather contradictory that we were going off to liberate Kuwait—and we have people in this country who don't have their civil liberties. We were damning Saddam Hussein for his use of violence and military force when we in turn just did the same thing.

—TRACY CHAPMAN, on the
Gulf War, 1992

I have a line [in one of my songs] that goes, "We've got a million rockers on call"—in other words, let's give Russia the feeling that America is unified and act like we're gonna stand behind this country and live and die by the American way.

—SAMMY HAGAR, of Van Halen

I'm tired of feeling like America has to be sorry for the things it's done. . . . Reagan, so what if he's a trigger-happy cowboy? He hasn't pulled the trigger. Don't you think it's better that Russia and all these other countries think he's a trigger-happy cowboy than think it's Jimmy Carter who wants to give them back the Panama Canal?

—NEIL YOUNG

I say what I believe at the time. It may not be the same in four years.

—NEIL YOUNG, defending his pro-Reagan,
pro-arms build-up statements in the '80s, 1995

Our fathers fought the wonderful war [World War II] to make the world safe for democracy and hot homemade pie, and we got stuck with the Vietnam ugliness, where the issues weren't cut and dried. That was the monkey wrench tossed into the mechanism of our spirit as a nation. They threw the American flag in our faces, saying, "Well, it's time for you guys to take up guns and go to war." Like taking a number in a deli. So we did it, and what did we get for the misery? Isolation from ourselves.

—BILLY JOEL, 1982

It was a war where for the first time people questioned the adage, "My country, right or wrong."   —STING, on the Vietnam War

I think it's a really false belief when they tell you, "Your country needs you." Yeah! A great nonsense, isn't it? They only need you as long as they've got a particular function for you. It's not your country—it doesn't belong to me.   —ELVIS COSTELLO, 1983

Our government can decide who they think should die—but does that make it right? I can go to war and kill, but if somebody attacked my mother and I went after them I could end up in prison for the rest of my life. And I could visualize the reasoning of doing that. The war, I don't even know why I'm over there.

—ICE-T, 1991

[Woodstock] was wonderful. I mean, it wasn't any fucking revolution; it was a three-day period during which people were decent to one another because they realized that if they weren't, they'd all get hungry.   —JOAN BAEZ

If I was 17 back in 1969, I wouldn't have gone to Woodstock. I would have gone to Detroit.
—KIM THAYIL, of Soundgarden, 1997

When we flew in and saw the mass of people sitting on the side of the hill, it was a frightful sight. It was like an army. There were two ways to look at this thing. There was the serious political side, which was kind of beautiful in that everybody wanted to join together like this; it was a very warm feeling. And then there was the other side, which was kind of frightening—this ripped army of mud people out there.

—ROBBIE ROBERTSON, of the Band, on
Woodstock, 1989

Too many people read serious political and sociological meanings into [Woodstock], way beyond its significance. I think it was a pretty innocent gathering from my point of view.

—COUNTRY JOE, 1989

I tried being a hippie for a year—it was a total loss. I was a lousy hippie.   —BILLY JOEL

Soon the new generation will rebel against me just like I rebelled against the older generation.   —BOB DYLAN

I do not cling to this antiquated hippie mentality that says it's us against them. . . . This is the age of adult rock stars. You can't be James Dean all your life.   —GLENN FREY, of the Eagles

I wonder what's happened to the '60s generation, the baby boomers who were going to change the country. We let it slip through our fingers somewhere along the line.

—DON HENLEY

I think a lot of the precepts of the late 1960s and early 1970s were based on just bullshit, concepts that don't exist. I don't think open relationships are part of human nature, I don't think open marriages have anything to do with human nature, I don't think drugs expand your consciousness. I think those things are dangerous and corrosive.   —TANYA DONELLY, of Belly

I'm usually good about my temper, but all these men trying to control women's bodies are really beginning to piss me off. They're talking from a bubble. They're not talking from the street, and they're not in touch with what's real. Well, I'm fucking mean, and I'm ugly and my name is reality.   —EDDIE VEDDER, of Pearl Jam, addressing the abortion issue at a concert in Pensacola, Florida, where Dr. David Gunn was shot to death in front of an abortion clinic, 1994

Abortion? I personally don't think abortion is that important. I think it's just an issue to evade whatever issues are makin' people think about abortion.   —BOB DYLAN

I'm not saying this because I'm looking for a soft cushion wherever I'm heading. I just feel that I've got thousands and thousands of young fans that have to learn about what's real when it comes to AIDS. Like the others before me, I would like to turn my own problems into something good that will reach out to all my homeboys and their kin, because I want to save their asses before it's too late. I'm not looking to blame anyone except myself. I've learned in the last week that this is real and it doesn't discriminate. It affects everyone.

—EAZY-E (1963–1995), from a statement he issued during the final days before his AIDS-related death, 1995

When Magic Johnson came forth with the fact that he'd contracted the HIV virus, it still kind of felt like that happened on an upscale level. You couldn't really see his lifestyle. Magic was just large, a basketball star. Eazy? His situation really hits home. He's a hardcore, hip-hop, gansta rapper who's around. This is a serious wake-up for everybody.

—TREACH, of Naughty by Nature, reacting to Eazy-E's announcement that he had AIDS, 1995

AIDS is a form of terrorism.
—YOKO ONO

Anyone will tell you that it's enormously energy inefficient. It goes: Forest is replaced by cow, cow is eaten by a person, then a person shits. A perfect way to turn foliage into feces.

—ROBYN HITCHCOCK, on why he doesn't eat beef, 1994

I'm sure if there's a new fascism, it won't come from skinheads and punks. It will come from people who eat granola and believe they know how the world should be.

—BRIAN ENO, record producer

They're silly people—Tipper Gore, especially. She's just a twit, a total twit. It's something to point their finger at. I mean, it's just like saying Anti-Christ/Devil-Child was the initials of AC/DC and we said, "Who thought of that?" That was amazing, we couldn't have thought of that ourselves. Sick fuck.

—BRIAN JOHNSON, of AC/DC, on activists who want to put warning labels on "R-rated" records, 1995

I'm a fairly with-it person, but this stuff is curling my hair.

—TIPPER GORE, on the need for cleaning up rock 'n' roll

This is about freezing people. If you listen to what they're really saying, their objective is to purge the entertainment industry of people whose ideas they disagree with. I find that morally repugnant.

—DAVE MARSH, rock journalist, on those in favor of censoring albums

In the Top 40, half the songs are secret messages to the teen world to drop out, turn on, and groove with the chemicals and light shows at discotheques.

—ART LINKLETTER, '50s TV personality

make me wanna holler

as usual, black music leads the world's pop music. They've always been ten years ahead of everyone else, always will be.

—JOHN PAUL JONES,
of Led Zeppelin, 1995

I mean, there is a sense of guilt, all white musicians feel that sense of guilt, that sense of duty to the black man, and whenever we meet black musicians, y'know, we're interested in what they think of us. —STING

A lot of people say, "What are you complaining about? Talking Heads has all these black members. Sting's band has a lot of black people in it." But essentially, these people are employees. It's really good that good musicians are getting work. But even though what Sting did was pretty nervy for him, those guys in his band were still in the background. I don't want to be the guy who is brought in to add some funk to the proceedings, to add some soul to the mix.

—VERNON REID, of Living Colour, 1987

Everyone says we're one black guy in an all-white band, but that's not true—we're actually three white guys in an all-black band.

—JIM SONEFELD,
of Hootie & the Blowfish, 1995

I always wanted a band that was black and white. Half of the musicians I knew only listened to one type of music. That wasn't good enough for me. —PRINCE

It's hard to imagine someone being racist. . . . [Without black music] we wouldn't have any of the music that we love. We'd be all these tight-assed WASPs doing jigs.

—LOU REED

It has to come across to the masses. Black people cannot feel Tracy Chapman, if they got beat over the head with it 35,000 times. I like to take what Tracy Chapman is about, but only once my mother-fucking funk is in place, because if you don't have your funk in place, you're not going to get over to the masses.

—CHUCK D, 1989

Being a black musician, you have that in you. It's like—no matter what you play—the funk always seems to slip through.

—LENNY KRAVITZ, 1995

All blacks don't sing the blues, all blacks don't play basketball, and all blacks don't dance.

—LIONEL RICHIE, responding to the accusation that his music lacks soul or funk, 1983

People [were] telling me, "You gotta do something that's funky, you gotta play funk." People [were] telling me my music wasn't black enough. That was weird. Because I am a black person, aren't I? Where I'm coming from is black. I relate to music that way, as opposed to straightening my hair and going through all that thing. This is me.

—VERNON REID, of Living Colour, 1987

When people try to put me down by saying things like "Black people can't sing rock 'n' roll," it just lights a fire in me. I say, wait a minute, we can all do all of it. If the Bee Gees can have an R&B hit, I can do rock or country, if I want to make the effort. This is music, and people are going to relate to it emotionally no matter where they are coming from; they don't have to even understand the words.

—DONNA SUMMER

There's a void. We have no Jaggers and no Rod Stewarts. We have a lot of groups that get up and put on costumes and go out and do Bojangles. Stepin Fetch[it] steps. That day is over. That choreography crap is over. Those kinds of groups do their routines, sing their falsettos and their little leads, and after that there's nothing. Black people don't want to be funkatized by groups up there dancing and wearing suits and bow ties and lickin' their eyebrows.

—RICK JAMES

I'm just lucky to be living at a time when black music—black romantic music—is riding high. But when you look back at history, black music has always led the way. I'm privileged to be part of that tradition.

—BABYFACE

I've developed this strong feeling about what's happening to so-called "primitive" and ethnic tribal peoples. I believe that the complexity of their music stands as a symbol of the richness of their societies, and I hope that people, upon listening to this music, might think that if these cultures can produce music this intricate and this intelligent, then they can't really be "primitive."

—BRIAN ENO, record producer

When I was a little girl, I wished I was black. . . . But if being black is synonymous with having soul, then yes, I feel that I am [black].

—MADONNA, 1987

After all, I am the last white nigger.

—PATTI SMITH, 1976

Although I'm a white, European, very English sort of person, I do understand and love the rhythms of black music.

—BRIAN FERRY, of Roxy Music, 1985

I have never considered it a disadvantage to be a black woman. I never wanted to be anything else. We have brains. We are beautiful. We can do anything we set our minds to.

—DIANA ROSS

We all live in a negative society that's always telling us we can't do this or that. Me being a black dude, I especially was always hearing that. "Color's always gonna stand in your way." I never believed that. Everything I dream of I can make a reality.

—MAURICE WHITE, of Earth, Wind
& Fire, 1976

You come into this place an uncorrupted person. I was little, but I remember the first experience of having my color thrown back at me and the state of shock it put me in.

—NENEH CHERRY

As long as you remain black, you're still
gonna be a nigga.
—EAZY-E (1963–1995)

I know how black people think and I also know how white people think. And in my book, you're white if you think the system is working for you. If you don't, you're black, whether you know it or not.

—ICE-T, 1991

Shit goin' the way it is—diseases, niggas gettin' killed, drugs, niggas poor—this shit is gonna cease. I feel it coming soon. Something's gonna trigger it. If I can trigger it, I'll trigger it myself. But it's time for this shit to stop.

—PRODIGY, of Mobb Deep, 1995

They killed Martin [Luther King], they killed Malcolm [X]. You got two black folk representing us through the '60s. One of them was for violence, and one was against it, and they both are dead. What is that saying? That's saying America doesn't give a fuck about a black motherfucker. Nigger, you're outta here when we say you're outta here. That's it.

—SNOOP DOGGY DOGG, 1995

There's two niggas inside me. One wants to live in peace, and the other won't die unless he's free.

—TUPAC SHAKUR (1971–1996), 1996

I believe that there's always gonna be some form of racism—as much as we'd like there to be peace—because people are different. Black culture is different.

—AXL ROSE, of Guns N' Roses, 1992

One of the problems in the United States is that "united in our prejudices we stand," you know? What unites people, very often, is their fear. —BRUCE SPRINGSTEEN

Music is one of the ways that we can combat racism. —PETER GABRIEL, 1986

[Jimi Hendrix] had to become white because it's a white tradition to do high art and Jimi was really into poetry. —PATTI SMITH, 1976

I could never be a racist. I love all the races of people, from Arabs to Jewish people. . . . My accountants and lawyers are Jewish. —MICHAEL JACKSON, responding to the suggestion that the phrase "kyke me" in one of his songs is anti-Semitic, 1995

Some of our economic policies are a real indirect kind of racism in which the people that get affected most are black people who are at the lower end of the economic spectrum. —BRUCE SPRINGSTEEN

Nobody cared about the [Los Angeles] riot until they thought it might spill into their nice neighborhoods. Then they got scared and called the National Guard. When it was in my hood, the police didn't give a fuck. When the looting was going on, the police ran right past. You saw it on TV: Everybody was running out of the stores and the police weren't doing shit. But when it spread to Beverly Hills, the police started beating motherfuckers. —SNOOP DOGGY DOGG, 1995

I don't give a fuck what color you are. The color of money is green. —EAZY-E (1963–1995)

Black male acts are far, far too apologetic. . . . Look, any black act in the States who has been [a] massive quote-unquote crossover success has had to emasculate himself to some degree. Prince has had to play the bisexual image, cast aspersions as to his dominant heterosexuality, [Michael] Jackson's had to be asexual, [Luther]

Vandross couldn't possibly offend anybody. . . . It's like in the contract, it certifies them to a free plastic surgeon visitation, guarantees them a makeup artist at all times to lighten 'em up for photographs.

—TERENCE TRENT D'ARBY

It's like the early days of rock 'n' roll. The authorities paid no attention as long as it was a black thing, but as soon as white kids began aping black styles, they came down hard.

—LUTHER CAMPBELL, of 2 Live Crew,
whose rap group has been the focus of the music
censorship crusade

There are too many barriers that keep blacks out of rock. . . . Rock stars are kids' heroes and I don't think a lot of parents in Wyoming and Montana want pictures of black rock singers in their kids' bedrooms. It's too threatening.   —RICK JAMES

If I could find a white man who had the Negro sound and Negro feel, I could make a billion dollars.

—SAM PHILLIPS, the man who discovered
Elvis Presley

The colored folk been singing it and playing it just the way I'm doin' now, man, for more years than I know. Nobody paid it no mind till I goosed it up.   —ELVIS PRESLEY (1935–1977), 1957

You know where Elvis got that from—he used to be down on Beale Street in Memphis. That's where he saw the black people doin' that. Ain't no way they'd let anybody like us get on TV and do that, but he could 'cause he's white.   —RAY CHARLES, on Presley's signature pelvic
gyrations, 1973

At least the Beatles did mention where they were influenced. They were great writers, on their own, but they did study black music.

—MICHAEL JACKSON, 1989

When we played the south, we had to get used to the fact that sometimes we'd have to give one show for white audiences and another for black. And we were good enough to perform in some clubs, but not good enough to stay there for the night, or even to shower there. —GLADYS KNIGHT

My thing was if I have to go into the [white] community . . . and I can only use the toilet in the back, I can only go in the back door of the restaurant, fine, fuck it—if that's the way you want it, it's your restaurant . . . but you cannot tell me if I play my music for you I got to make my people sit in the back. I won't do that. My people made me, and I cannot deal with the fact that they cannot sit anywhere they want to sit.

—RAY CHARLES, on playing the segregated
South in the '50s

The first words I learned to read were "White Only" and "Black Only." —CYRIL NEVILLE, of the Neville Brothers

They record the song and the white stations start playing it. It's the same song, but they call me "rhythm and blues," and they call the white boy "rock 'n' roll." Just so long as it was separate, they could make believe it wasn't a black record anymore. But it *was* written by a black dude—me. —BO DIDDLEY

You still see a lot of prejudices or racism in the music industry. A lot of radio stations don't play music for what it is, so you still have your black radio stations and your white radio stations; this one will play rock and this one wants to play hip-hop or funk and another one don't want to play nothing at all but Top 40. If things don't change for the better, the 1990s are gonna be hell.

—AFRIKA BAMBAATAA, 1989

Black executives, they get invited to the golf tournaments. I don't give a fuck about all that. I'm not gonna play golf with you. When you're playin' golf, I'm [gonna] be in the studio. While you trying to eat dinner with the other executives in the business, I'm [gonna] be havin' dinner with my family, which is the artists on the label. Without your talent, *you ain't shit.*

—SUGE KNIGHT, CEO of Death Row
Records, whose artists include Tupac Shakur
and Dr. Dre, 1996

In the '50s, they were able to separate rock 'n' roll into white and black. Now here comes rap: It's a rock attitude again, and white kids are like, "Yo, this is kind of different." It's eliminating a lot of stereotypes about black people that their mothers taught 'em. That's why this whole censorship thing is bullshit. It's not about fear of them liking Ice-T. . . . It's fear of a black icon. Now you see kids with African pendants and stuff.

—ICE-T, 1991

> I guarantee you, Nat King Cole go down there
> in Alabama [in the 1950s] and sing these love songs,
> and they'd beat him up.
> —RAY CHARLES

"Tutti Frutti" really started the races being together. Because when I was a boy, the white people would sit upstairs. They called it "white spectators," and the blacks was downstairs. And the white kids would jump over the balcony and come down where I was and dance with the blacks. We started that merging all across the country. From the git-go, my music was accepted by whites.

—LITTLE RICHARD, 1990

In my early days in radio I would think that 50 percent of my audience was white—high school kids who were crazy about R&B music. At the shows they could sit upstairs and watch the black kids downstairs having a good time dancing. They just had to sit up there and watch. —HAMP SWAIN, DJ credited with discovering Otis Redding

We used to get letters from kids in Grosse Point and the white areas around Detroit saying, "I sneaked and bought your record, I really liked it. What else do you have coming out on your label? My parents won't let me have them." —SMOKEY ROBINSON

When I was really young, I couldn't tell the difference between black music, rockabilly and rock 'n' roll. . . . I dug 'em all. I really couldn't tell the difference between 'em. All I knew was if the music implied toughness, hardness, or badass on any level, then I liked it.

—MICHAEL BLOOMFIELD (1943–1981)

Musically, I lived in the best of both worlds. I hated it that you had to choose which field you were in because of the color of your skin. At one point, for the first two or three years after we made it, we were listed as Rhythm & Blues artists, which I thought was really incredible. We bridged that gap.

—DON EVERLY, of the Everly Brothers

You know, there's this place where a river runs into an ocean and the fresh water and the salt water all get mixed in together. And that's what America is all about, and that's what American music is about and that's what rock 'n' roll is about. It actually wasn't invented by anybody, and it's not just black and white, either. It's Mexican and Appalachian and Gaelic and everything that's come floating down the river.

—T-BONE BURNETT

When I first went to New York in 1951, I went to see an arranger who I really adored. . . . And he said, ". . . I'm the greatest Negro arranger in the United States." And it shocked me, because that's not what I wanted to be. That was exactly what I didn't want to be. I wanted to be the greatest arranger in the world, man. . . . I thought, "What the fuck is that? You got twelve notes. Those notes don't know the difference who's using them. Some of 'em are white, some of 'em are black."

—QUINCY JONES, record producer, 1995

We all come from a slave singing out in a field somewhere.

—LENNY KRAVITZ, 1995

unk rock is a totally liberating genre. There's the kitchen sink—and you can throw anything you want into it. —THURSTON MOORE, of Sonic Youth, 1994

Punk rock is my race, man. It's the color of my skin.

—LARS FREDERICKSEN, of Rancid, 1995

Punk rock has existed throughout the history of rock 'n' roll, they just didn't call it that. In the '50s, when rock 'n' roll was . . . new . . . the media had a field day. This stuff was derided mercilessly, it was called "unmusical," it was blamed for juvenile delinquency, sexual depravity . . . if not the demise of Western civilization as a whole. It was said that the musicians could not play their instruments. . . . It was said that the singers could not sing. . . . It was written off nearly everywhere as a load of garbage that would come and go within a year's time, a fad like the hula hoop. Is any of this beginning to sound vaguely familiar? —LESTER BANGS (1949–1982), rock journalist, 1980

Punks should have no politics or be right-wing; otherwise they're just hippies dressed as punks. . . . Punks should stand on the street corner and do nothing, like Marlon Brando in *The Wild One.*

—JOHNNY RAMONE, of the Ramones, 1983

It wasn't so much violent as anarchic. Punk rock was mostly just uprising, about expressing yourself, with dance and fashion and style. Rebellion. You go left, I go right.

—DR. KNOW, of Bad Brains, 1995

The key word—to me anyway—in the punk definition was "a beginner, an inexperienced hand." Punk rock—any kid can pick up a guitar and become a rock 'n' roll star, despite or because of his lack of ability, talent, intelligence . . . and usually does so out of frustration, hostility, a lot of nerve and a need for ego fulfillment.

—PETER CROWLEY, music journalist and critic, 1976

That's my definition of punk rock. A newborn baby crying.

—THURSTON MOORE, of Sonic Youth, 1994

We may not have anarchy in the streets, but at least we can have it in our little club [of punks].　—SIOUXSIE SIOUX, of Siouxsie and the Banshees, 1976

Punk was rebellious—and justified in that response—but it had very little to do with music, and so it created a highly charged but frighteningly floundering atmosphere that I found very, very disheartening. . . . Punk seemed like rock 'n' roll music utterly without the music.　—STEVE WINWOOD, 1989

Everyone I know is so sick of all the punk violence and pessimism. Anyway, the truth is that it's so much harder to write a pop song that everyone can relate to than some anthem of hate for a few punks.　—BOY GEORGE

All these alternative bands today are so high up on their punk-rock horse that they're in denial about being huge and playing big shows. Not only do we respect the clichés, we see truth in them. So we simultaneously make fun of them and embrace them.

—BILLY CORGAN, of the Smashing Pumpkins

I think it's really weird. There are all these bands that are punk and confess a punk ethic and they're going for the big dollars. It's unbelievable. We are now living in a world of millionaire punks.

—JOHNNY RZEZNIK, of Goo Goo Dolls, 1995

The hardcore punk scene is so elitist. The feeling is that not everybody is "good enough" to listen to this music. I've never understood that attitude, because I've always thought that everyone should get an even chance to hear our music. Don't you want as many people as possible to relate to what you're doing?

—NOODLES, of the Offspring, 1995

I don't know what all this '90s bollocks is about! Some journalists in America get upset because they think Green Day and Rancid are punk, but to me, punk existed from 1976 to '79. Punks today are kind of sad. —EDWIN COLLINS, 1995

What I've been hearing is a lot of music that sounds like certain songs that I've written, only with big, radio-friendly production and phony British accents. There are people who actually get into the music and realize what we've contributed to it, but your average mall punk or some jock who happens to hear an Offspring record, they're not going to put that together.

—BILL STEVENSON, of Black Flag, on the
'90s punk revival

[Punk rock] is not what it was in 1977 and anybody who is old enough to remember knows the difference. It's being heralded as a new movement, and we know it's bogus.

—BILLY CORGAN, of the Smashing
Pumpkins, 1995

There's a punk-rock kid on every corner today. Everyone now is kind of spoon-fed. Back when we started, it was very underground. We had to struggle and scamper just to play anywhere we could play and open the doors for all these other [punk] bands.

—KEITH MORRIS, of Circle Jerks, 1995

Whatever happened to all the punk bands? All the bands that we opened for and played with: Black Flag, Minutemen, Youth Brigade, Seven Seconds, Hüsker Dü, Effigies, all the fucking hardcore bands. There isn't a damn one of them left. We fucking outlasted the whole stinking lot of posers, and all the time they gave us shit for having plaid shirts and hair.

—PAUL WESTERBERG,
of the Replacements, 1989

These kids don't know about us or bands like us. It's not really their fault per se, but they've gotta go back and check their roots. . . . The kids need a little history lesson, that's all.

—DR. KNOW, of Bad Brains, on the relative obscurity of the first punk bands, 1995

Here in the U.K. the legacy of punk is incredible. You get talk show hosts who were punks, a lot of our top comedians, film makers, writers, artists used to be punks.

—MIKE JONES, of the Clash

It's strange. What was left of center is now the center. I guess that's why it's time for folk records again. The most punk-rock thing you could do now is make a folk record.

—RICK RUBIN, record producer, 1995

Women
in Rock

i want to be the girl with the most cake

Playing guitar is a sexual thing. It comes from the crotch, it comes from the heart, and it comes from the head—you don't need to have muscles to play it. I'd love to see even more women pick up the instrument—besides, it's cool now to have a girl in your band.

—LITA FORD, 1995

What if a little girl picked up a guitar and said "I wanna be a rock star." Nine times out of ten her parents would never allow her to do it. We don't have so many lead guitar women, not because women don't have the ability to play the instrument, but because they're kept locked up, taught to be something else. I don't appreciate that.

—DAVID LEE ROTH

I like being in a position of, you know, Mom with a guitar.

—TANYA DONELLY, of Belly, 1995

Well, I was a girl with a guitar, you know.

—JONI MITCHELL, on how she got her folksinger label, 1995

I'm actually surprised whenever I read [about] women talking about how tough it is to be in rock. . . . You definitely have specific problems as a woman in the music industry, but I'm not sure they aren't any more or less true of being a woman in general.

—JUSTINE FRISCHMANN, of Elastica, 1995

I had one journalist ask me about rock 'n' roll being a male energy, and I said "Well, I'm female," and he said, "But you're a lesbian!"

—MELISSA ETHERIDGE, 1994

[My look] is a more androgynous portrayal, but it isn't meant to be butch. No way. It *is* very useful in transcending the bum-and-tits things, though. That's a very vulgar thing to say, but I have received that kind of abuse onstage, and one has to find a way around it. Of course, you'll never find a way around it. But this helps.

—ANNIE LENNOX, 1983

Rock 'n' roll is a very butch thing, and it appeals to one hard side of the masculine character. But I don't think the Rolling Stones are only a rock band. They can be other things. They can be very feminine.

—MICK JAGGER, 1994

For a while it was assumed that I was writing women's songs. Then men began to notice that they saw themselves in the songs, too. A good piece of art should be androgynous. I'm not a feminist. That's too divisional for me.

—JONI MITCHELL

I realized I'd found a female audience, just by being honest. Not necessarily by saying, "I am gay, I am gay, I am gay." But just by being honest about the fact that I understand how gay people feel, and I identify. And I know how it feels to be a woman. I know how it feels to be a woman because I am a woman. And I won't be classified as just a man.

—PETE TOWNSHEND, 1989

I do think women play differently to men. I think they do less guitar leads for one, which drive me up the wall. Women put less of that widdly show-off stuff into their songs—like "This is how fast I can go!" Who said fast was good anyway?

—KAT BJELLAND, of Babes in Toyland, 1994

Rock 'n' roll is for men. Real rock 'n' roll is a man's job. I want to see a man up there. I want to see a man's muscles, a man's veins. I don't want to see no chick's tit banging against a bass.

—PATTI SMITH

I hate to see chicks perform. Hate it. . . . Because they whore them-selves. Especially the ones that don't wear anything. They fuckin' whore themselves. —BOB DYLAN, 1987

How many girls other than Bonnie Raitt can play a guitar solo? I can't, you know. I haven't seen any female guitar players that are really anything special. —JULIANA HATFIELD (She has since recanted this remark.)

Unfortunately, women are treated like giraffes or something in music. It's still strange to see one on stage in 1994 which I think is ridiculous. —TANYA DONELLY, of Belly, 1994

There's really no reason to have women on tour, unless they've got a job to do. The only other reason is to screw. Otherwise, they get bored. They just sit around and moan.

—MICK JAGGER

And it was exciting to be there in the wake of the comet of the Rolling Stones. It was very interesting and I wouldn't have missed it for anything. But I was in the classic feminine position. I was the clever beautiful woman behind the great man.

—MARIANNE FAITHFUL, describing her relationship with Mick Jagger, 1994

I don't like categorizing stuff, but women's roles all through history have been to act as hierophant or someone who's guarded the secrets or guarded the temple. I'm a girl doing what guys usually did, the way I look, the goals and kinds of things I want to achieve through rock. It's more heroic stuff and heroic stuff has been tradi-tionally male. —PATTI SMITH, 1976

Liz Phair, Juliana Hatfield, Belly, the Breeders—all these amazing women who are just rocking: Their companies don't want them to be considered rock 'n' roll. —MELISSA ETHERIDGE

After [the Go-Gos] sold three or four million albums, we thought we wouldn't be treated like an all-girl band anymore, but as a rock 'n' roll band. That never really worked.

—BELINDA CARLISLE

I didn't even think about being a woman until I started getting interviewed. . . . I have never felt unequal to men. If anything I felt stronger than them. —KAT BJELLAND, of Babes in Toyland, 1994

I'm telling you right fucking now, women are the superior beings on the planet. Women teach more about things than we'll ever know. . . . When you really begin to trust a woman with your life is when men become men. —ED KOWALCZYK, of Live, 1996

I think women rule the world and that no man has ever done anything that a woman either hasn't allowed him to do or encouraged him to do. —BOB DYLAN, 1984

From the time I was seven or eight, I was a tomboy. . . . Well, I just couldn't stand the way girls got the second best of everything. They couldn't throw as far. They weren't paid as much. To me, it was the same as black people getting treated as second-class citizens. —BONNIE RAITT, 1990

I've always been a tomboy. I used to go to the extreme of trying to go to the loo like boys and wetting my pants in the process when I was three. It just didn't make sense, being a girl.
—DOLORES O'RIORDAN,
of the Cranberries, 1995

I think the older I get the more I cherish the good qualities that go along with being a woman. I think for so long there, being a woman was almost synonymous with being a scrapper in this business. And a certain amount of that is really good; I think you do have to scrap to get your voice heard, and that forces you to commit to your ideals. —SHERYL CROW, 1995

I have these weird latent misogynist tendencies. A lot of women put themselves in the position where they can play the dependent or weak person. I think that women should try to be in good shape. Women should be as strong as they can, because they're naturally weaker. —JULIANA HATFIELD

Women are absolutely equal. They just can't lift as much.
—DAVID LEE ROTH, 1988

"Girls Just Want to Have Fun" doesn't mean "Girls Just Want to Fuck." —CYNDI LAUPER

Don't think that sticking your boobs out and trying to look fuckable will help. Remember you're in a rock 'n' roll band. It's not "fuck me," it's "fuck you!" —CHRISSIE HYNDE's advice to female rockers

I like music that's warm and has a female point of view, but also has passion and sexuality. Feminists have always said women should be all of those things. If you listen to Etta James or Mavis Staples, they were doing that all along. —JOAN OSBORNE, 1995

I get so much bad press for being overtly sexual. When someone like Prince, Elvis, or Jagger does the same things, they are being honest sexual human beings. But when I do it: "Oh, please, Madonna, you're setting the woman's movement back a million years."
—MADONNA, 1985

How can you criticize a woman for having a sexuality when men for years and years have been singing about nothing else?
—CYNDI LAUPER

I seriously think that in rock 'n' roll, if you're a woman and you've got two arms and two legs, you're bound to be considered a sex symbol.
—JUSTINE FRISCHMANN, of Elastica, 1996

I think women like me because they don't have to be jealous. I'm not ridiculously beautiful, and I'm not wealthy, and I'm not intimidatingly talented. I'm probably as close to a normal person as you'll find in the music business. —BONNIE RAITT

I know I come off lookin' like a fuckin' haggy housewife compared to all these other women in rock, and that's fine with me, man. So I don't wanna wash my hair, fuck you, this is how I look.
—KIM DEAL, of the Breeders, 1995

If women could learn to be as unattractive as men, it would go a long way toward demystifying females in bands.

—TANYA DONELLY, of Belly, 1994

Women are just not allowed to be characters. A man is allowed to be scruffy or a hunk, or Woody Allen or Albert Einstein, and still be accepted as 100 percent man. But if a woman hasn't got a certain figure or doesn't make an effort to remain on a level which is considered feminine, she isn't in the game.

—BJÖRK, 1994

Some of these feminists become fascists, because they're saying if I don't do certain things that they deem appropriate then I'm not a strong independent woman. Bullshit!

—TORI AMOS, 1994

So maybe I scare men away.

—JOAN BAEZ, 1983

You're running into a whole different woman these days. There's now a lot of masculinity amongst the female gender.

—ERIC CLAPTON, 1989

People really aren't used to women expressing the kinds of things we do. Just because I'm screaming doesn't mean I'm screaming out of anger. I could be screaming out of passion or frustration.

—KAT BJELLAND, of Babes in
Toyland, 1994

There's this kind of feeling that now it's men who are oppressed!

—MARIANNE FAITHFUL, 1994

Well, I think birth control is another hoax that women shouldn't have bought, but they did. I mean, if a man don't wanna knock up a woman, that's his problem, you know what I mean? It's interesting: They arrest prostitutes, but they never arrest the guys with the prostitutes. —BOB DYLAN

The pill turned women into men. Men can afford to go around and fuck every night, but women can't. Women have to go by their own cycle, you know? I'm very governed by my cycle. And I think that to take a pill, and to turn yourself into a robot, and fuck every night like a man, it's . . . it's what it does to your intuitive psyche. A woman's gotta stay home some nights. If she doesn't want to get pregnant, she doesn't fuck, period. And if a guy that she loves wants to fuck someone, he's gonna have to go off and fuck someone else that night, and she's gonna have to put up with it.
—CHRISSIE HYNDE, of the Pretenders, 1980

This isn't a dig on women, but I think women are so different chemically from men, and that makes it hard to sustain a relationship. They have periods, they go through horrible, awful emotional swings, and trying to be logical with a person that's got a whole different logic running around in her brain is just impossible.
—LAYNE STALEY, of Alice in Chains, 1996

I've been doing a lot of [therapy] and found out I've had a lot of hatred for women. —AXL ROSE, of Guns N' Roses, 1992

I see women more and more as friends, and less and less as candidates for sexual domination. —STING, 1987

I love doing anything with women. . . . I prefer the company of women to men, for a start. I think that usually when I meet a female that I get on very well with, something creative seems to take place. —ERIC CLAPTON, 1989

You can learn a lot about a woman by getting smashed with her.
—TOM WAITS

Sometimes a woman can really persuade you to make an asshole of yourself. —ROD STEWART

Art & the Music

talk about the
passion

rust the art, not the artist.
— BRUCE SPRINGSTEEN, 1984

I'm an artist, and if you give me a tuba, I'll bring something out of it.
— JOHN LENNON (1940–1980), 1971

You give me a fucking kazoo and I'll write you a good song.
— BILLY CORGAN, of the Smashing Pumpkins, 1995

A lot of artists have one way of art and another way of life: in me, they're the same.
— JANIS JOPLIN (1943–1970)

My work is not me. Creating is a touching thing, it's a hurting thing. You're trying to discover how you really regard things and there's pain in that, an intensity, because with that recognition as the starting point, you're then trying to make something that is extra to yourself, that is better than yourself.
— BRYAN FERRY, of Roxy Music, 1985

We're talking art's artifice here, and it has its own truth. It's not necessarily a literal truth. It's a creative truth, a larger truth.
— JONI MITCHELL, 1988

Fear and greed are not good bases for a creative artist to work from.
— JOE JACKSON

Artists everywhere steal mercilessly all the time and I think this is healthy.
— PETER GABRIEL

Well, I think "great art" is a pompous phrase. To me, that's a little tough to swallow, and it's tough to spit out, too.

—JAMES TAYLOR, 1979

But it's not what you actually put on the canvas, it's the reason why you did it. Like the Andy Warhol thing. It wasn't why he painted a Campbell's soup can. It was "What sort of man paints a Campbell's soup can?" That's what aggravates people.

—DAVID BOWIE, 1976

Art is sufficiently broad that if you want to lie on the floor and wriggle like a snake, that's art. —PAUL McCARTNEY, 1987

Great paintings shouldn't be in museums. Museums are cemeteries. Paintings should be on the walls of restaurants, in dime stores, in gas stations, in men's rooms. . . . It's not the bomb that has to go, man, it's the museums. —BOB DYLAN

I believe that a performer sometimes lives in this netherworld for the benefit of those who can't go there; the listeners' lives are made richer by getting the feeling from the artist, but they can't join him at the source. —BRYAN FERRY, of Roxy Music, 1985

The friction is in living. In waking up every day. And getting through another day. That's where the friction is. And to express it in art is the job of the artist. And that's what I can do. To express it on behalf of the people who can't express it or haven't the time or ability or whatever it is. That's my job.

—JOHN LENNON (1940–1980)

I think the function of art is to reflect God and to try and remember all the knowledge that we had before we were born, of how powerful we are and what God is. I think that's the drive to create, to fill the space, to fill the emptiness, even for just two seconds, so as to achieve the sense of having reflected, or having opened up and connected with, whatever it is that is above us.

—SINÉAD O'CONNOR, 1992

As an audience, we look at a painting or hear the music and recognize truth of some kind that affects us deeply. It explains our universe to us in some way that is reassuring. It is that which makes me feel there may well be something to be in tune with.

—ROGER WATERS, of Pink Floyd, 1992

Although we have this divinity, or creativity, within us, it is covered with material energy, and a lot of the time our actions come from a mundane level. We're like beggars in the goldmine, where everything has really enormous potential and perfection, but we're all so ignorant with the dust of our desire on our mirrors.

—GEORGE HARRISON, 1992

I think you plug into this electricity. It's like a river in a way; no question. When the magic's there, everyone in the room feels it. You're a bit like a radio aerial and you quiver when you're on to something.

—PETER GABRIEL, on the creative spark, 1992

You can try to be a disciplined person and be in shape to handle inspiration when it happens. If you stand around looking for it, it never happens. . . . I think there is something like a current—to tell you the truth it's something I believe in without spending too much time thinking about it. Mainly I spend a lot of time standing in line trying to get a little of it, trying to tap into it.

—JACKSON BROWNE, 1992

I have to create. I have to dig in the earth; I have to make something grow; I have to bake something; I have to write something; I have to sing something; I have to put something out. It's not a need to prove anything. It's just my way of life.

—BETTE MIDLER

I love to create magic—to put something together that's so unusual, so unexpected that it blows people's heads off. Something ahead of the times. Five steps ahead of what people are thinking. So people see it and say, "Whoa! I wasn't expecting that!"

—MICHAEL JACKSON, 1982

I created, man. From listening to someone speak, the intonation of their voice, I could capture a line. I look at people walking and get a beat from their movement.

—JAMES JAMERSON, one of the originators
of the Motown sound

If anything is a big influence on me, it's David Lynch. He's really into presenting something but not explaining it. It's just "This is an image, this is an idea, isn't it cool?" The way I understand it, that's the only way to be surreal. To be not so connected with it, except that it came from your brain, somewhere way back there.

—FRANK BLACK, of the Pixies, 1989

good vibrations

In a weird kind of way, music has afforded me an idealism and perfectionism that I could never attain as me.

—BILLY CORGAN, of the Smashing Pumpkins, 1995

Your music is your ideals a lot of the time, and you don't live up to those ideals all the time. You try, but you fall short, and you disappoint yourself. —BRUCE SPRINGSTEEN, 1984

[Woody Guthrie, Lightnin' Hopkins, and Big Joe Williams] got to where music was a tool for them, a way to live more, a way to make themselves feel better. Sometimes I can make myself feel better with music, but other times it's still hard to go to sleep at night.

—BOB DYLAN

It's the music that kept us all intact . . . kept us from going crazy. You should have two radios in case one gets broken.

—LOU REED

If our motive is to instill good, positive, healing force in our music—something that will elevate the listener—then people can pick up on it in a sublime level. It doesn't matter what kind of music it is—it can be the most raucous thing in the world or just a couple of notes on a classical guitar.

—ERIC JOHNSON, 1995

Music is a spiritual doorway. . . . Its power comes from the fact that it plugs directly into the soul, unlike a lot of visual art or text information that has to go through the more filtering processes of the brain.　—PETER GABRIEL, 1992

When the real music comes to me—the music of the spheres, the music that surpasseth understanding—that has nothing to do with me, 'cause I'm just the channel. The only joy for me is for it to be given to me, and to transcribe it like a medium. . . . Those moments are what I live for.

—JOHN LENNON (1940–1980)

All music comes from a very pure place. There's a science to orchestrating, certain principles that are there, and then you have your gift on top of that. But with melody there are no principles, there is no science. All melodies come straight from God.

—QUINCY JONES, record producer, 1995

To me the most important thing about any musician is, can you walk in a bar and get a free drink with a song, you know?

—KEITH RICHARDS

But it's still the music that's special, not the musicians. We have to continue to get that across to ourselves as well as the audience.

—BONO, 1987

I think music should reflect its environment. A musician should be just as much a part of a community as a bricklayer or a shopkeeper.

—STUART ANDERSON, of Big Country

Nobody complains that you put paintings on your wall and they don't change. My reply is to treat music in the same way. It becomes a condition of your environment without demanding that you concentrate on it intensely.　—BRIAN ENO, record producer

People deserve better. They deserve truth. They deserve honesty. The best music . . . is essentially there to provide you something to face the world with.　—BRUCE SPRINGSTEEN

Music for me is order out of chaos, and the world is chaos.

—STING, 1987

Music needs to make sense, needs to have order. From what some people consider the lowest stuff—a cat in the middle of a cotton field shouting the blues—to what's considered the highest—a symphony or an opera—it has to be structured.

—RAY CHARLES

We try to subvert reality through music.

—BRIAN RITCHIE, of Violent Femmes, 1983

> **Music is forever; music should grow and mature with you, following you right up until you die.**
> —PAUL SIMON, 1975

Music is the timeless experience of constant change.

—JERRY GARCIA (1942–1995), of the
Grateful Dead

For me, music is this magic acoustic element that makes perfectly rational people who have come to realize the inalterable fact that they are truly alone in the world somehow feel for fleeting moments that maybe they're not [alone] after all. It's this pleasant, soothing vibration we can send out or take in that keeps us company. Chopin, Gershwin, the Beatles, the lyricism in their music chases that sadness, makes me feel like part of the human family. It's a chemical reaction of some sort. A very odd thing.

—BILLY JOEL, 1982

Music really is a way to reach out and hold on to each other in a healthy way. I'm finding that out now. It's helped me to open up more and take a chance on loving people, instead of just isolating [myself] and suspecting everybody I run into.

—STEVIE RAY VAUGHN (1954–1990)

Music has to get to the people. In the heart, in the head, I don't care where, so long as it fucking gets them!

—ELVIS COSTELLO

So often people try so hard in a cerebral way to create something new that they get away from the natural human function of music, which is to enliven the bodily fluids.

—FLEA, of Red Hot Chili Peppers, 1995

Truly, music is just feelings and I'm not trying to be philosophical or anything. That is the beauty of music, that it's down to earth and about really boring things like driving your car or taking the tube or doing an interview or anything.

—BJÖRK, 1994

I think music is way beyond rational thinking. It doesn't have to make any sense.

—MICHAEL STIPE, of R.E.M.

I had no intention of letting the music be anything other than troublesome to people. We really wanted to go out there and annoy people.

—JOHN CALE, of Velvet Underground

I do what I do because of the radio. Consider Devo: My, how artistic, what a great concept—deevolution and industrial rock for the '80s. But it doesn't make it on the radio. If I'm driving in my car, I'd rather hear Donna Summer—that's where it's at.

—BILLY JOEL, 1980

Many of the artists today don't really interpret anything. I mean, the Doors don't interpret. They're not interpreters of music. They sing ideas. The Beach Boys have always sung ideas—they've never been interpreters. The Beatles interpret; "Yesterday" meant something. Whereas "Good Vibrations" was a nice idea on which everyone sort of grooved.

—PHIL SPECTOR, record producer, 1969

Not always the most popular music satisfies the collective unconscious of the most people. Popular music is basically crass and appeals at a crass level. I think a lot of the less [commercially] successful writers are really tapping into the collective unconscious, but people won't realize it for another ten years or so. The audience is slightly behind. I don't think someone like Madonna taps into the collective unconscious.

—RICHARD THOMPSON, 1992

There's a lot of gloss, a lot of facade in music today. Fortunately, underneath the surface, there's good stuff going on, which supports the chrome up on top. People who are interested in music, or interested in what's being communicated, will always start out with the veneer and then dip down and find out what's underneath. They're the ones who will get the reward.

—ERIC CLAPTON, 1992

You must be inside of it, know what's happening to you, and why you want to play this music. You don't just go run and play this music. Because you think you can make a million off of it. But the music have to have a purpose.   —BOB MARLEY (1945–1981), 1975

The music I like most is done by people who convey a sense of self, a feeling that they'd continue making music even if they weren't making records. Music is a part of their lives, not just a vehicle to stardom.   —PETER BUCK, of R.E.M.

For me, music is a natural byproduct of living. It's an urge I get. I do it and I feel better. I usually don't think of it in terms of what I'm trying to achieve [commercially]. It's what I am, for better or worse.

—MATTHEW SWEET, 1995

What really excites me is music done by individuals who are basically trying to articulate their own personae, so it's music made by eccentrics, it isn't really designed to relate to a mass of people. . . . What I find most alarming is groups that are attempting to articulate the voice of a generation rather than their own.

—NICK CAVE

To be perfectly honest with you, I don't really follow what's going on in music. It's like if you work in a garage—you don't go home and fix your car.   —OZZY OSBOURNE, 1996

I don't listen to music. I hate music.

—JOHNNY ROTTEN, of the Sex Pistols

I don't know anything about music. In my line of work you don't have to.   —ELVIS PRESLEY (1935–1977)

I didn't think about choosing music as a career risk. There was no question because of my extreme dedication. I had to do it. I didn't think about it, I was desperate. I had to do it and nothing would stop me. . . . I guess that I was fortunate because I started making a living out of it, so I guess I'm lucky. Oh my God, I think I feel guilty again. —JULIANA HATFIELD, 1995

Music allowed me to eat. But it also allowed me to express myself. I played because I had to play. I rid myself of bad dreams and rotten memories. —PRINCE

There's a certain part of my brain that is just so devoted to music that it becomes a disabler. Remembering phone numbers is more difficult for me than the average person because I'm always trying to remember a melody I thought of earlier.
—DAVE PIRNER, of Soul Asylum, 1995

You get inside the music to such an extent that you kind of are the music, or the music's you. You're thinking about it but you're not thinking about it. Sometimes I think it's almost a flashing backwards and forwards of intellect and intuition. . . . You're just sort of flying along, and then you have another conscious moment.
—RICHARD THOMPSON, 1992

Everybody gives off a certain musical note. I think I'm F-sharp. The thing is you can go around and you meet somebody who's in F-sharp, you're in harmony, see. But if you meet somebody who's in F-unng, it's a discord: you don't get on.
—DONOVAN

Rhythm is something you either have or don't have, but when you have it, you have it all over. —ELVIS PRESLEY (1935–1977)

I had bought the idea that I was the Virgin Mary—I mean, I was very stuffy about my music. —JOAN BAEZ, 1983

My music is not disillusionary. It has something to say. It speaks the truth. If people don't like it, well, then they can go to hell.
—RICK JAMES

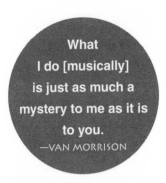

What I do [musically] is just as much a mystery to me as it is to you.
—VAN MORRISON

Magic is what we do. Music is the way we do it.
—JERRY GARCIA (1942–1995), of the
Grateful Dead, 1989

I don't think my music's weird. There's a fine line between being weird and trying to be weird. I just improvise and use the first thing that comes to mind. . . . Weird is happening in the '90s. It's a genre. But the '90s are too weird, so in the last two years I've been heading toward normal. That's gonna be the next radical thing. Soon normalcy will be the edge. —BECK, 1995

If I told you what our music is really about we'd probably all get arrested. —BOB DYLAN, 1965

Our music's kind of about taking something ugly and making it beautiful. —JERRY CANTRELL, of Alice in Chains, 1996

I believe my music is the healin' music. I believe my music can make the blind see, the lame walk, the deaf and dumb hear and talk, because it inspires and uplifts people. It regenerates the ears, makes the liver quiver, the bladder splatter, and the knees freeze. I'm not conceited, either. —LITTLE RICHARD

I'm not afraid to be the boss, see? That's how James Brown music came to be. Back when everybody was listening to soap-suds songs and jingles, I emphasized the beat, not the melody, understand? Heat the beat, and the rest'll turn sweet.
—JAMES BROWN, 1986

My [approach to music] is more visual than it is sound. I try to paint pictures with sound. In the beginning it feels like charcoal sketches, then pastel and watercolors as you start to figure out the contour and shape of it, its climaxes, its rises and falls. It has a shape just like a dramatic form, and you've got to make each climax a little higher. . . . It's like sex, you know.

—QUINCY JONES, record producer, 1995

My approach is jazz, as far as trying to leave enough space for something to happen in the music instead of trying to control it all the time. Leaving room for it to grow, give everybody some breathing space. —VAN MORRISON

The reason I latched on to this folk thing is, similarly to punk, it's of the people. It's subcorporate music. The whole problem with folk with me is, it's so folky. But then I show up at these folk festivals, and everybody's so laid-back, everybody's so unpretentious— as opposed to when I'm playing at rock festivals, and it's like "I would like to smile at you, but I'm trying to be really cool."

—ANI DiFRANCO, 1995

Folk music creates its own audience. Because you can take a guitar anywhere, anytime. —BOB DYLAN, 1987

while my guitar gently weeps

he guitar saved my life. I'd either be dead or in jail if I didn't have the guitar. It was always there. It was someone I could talk to. It was my lady. I could always go to it, and it would help me out. —MARC FORD, of the Black Crowes, 1995

The guitar is my first wife. She don't talk back; she talks *for* me. She don't scream at me; she screams *for* me—and she sho' do have a sweet tone when she do. —STEVIE RAY VAUGHN (1954–1990)

My guitar is the only thing in my life that hasn't fucked me over. —DAVE MUSTAINE, of Megadeth

I realized that the only way I was ever going to fit into society and have a role was with the guitar. —PETE TOWNSHEND

My first guitar was one of the most beautiful sights I'd ever seen in my life. It was a magic scene. There it is. The Guitar. It was real and it stood for something. "Now you're real." I had found a way to do everything I wanted to do. —BRUCE SPRINGSTEEN

I wouldn't necessarily say I had a direction or anything, I just knew I wanted to write songs. It wasn't any kind of cosmic force or anything like that. It was just a matter of having a guitar around and wanting to play it all the time. —BILLIE JOE ARMSTRONG, of Green Day

I just play what I feel like playing, and every once in a while I'll wake up and feel like playing something else.

—NEIL YOUNG, 1995

I think of myself as a piano player and songwriter; my singing is all tied to my piano playing. I do all my vocals live while I'm playing, which results in leakage between the vocal and piano mikes. There's never the total separation you'd get with a first-rate mix, but that's become an aspect of my sound, a distinctive trait. And if I must overdub sometime, I'll literally sit at the closed piano and pound my fingers on the lid. Guess the piano bone is connected to the throat bone.

—BILLY JOEL, 1982

I use piano wire for the guitar strings, 'cause it's a lot thicker. I buy it in bulk, in these big long tubes, and just cut it to the length of the guitar.

—KURT COBAIN (1967–1994), of Nirvana

One guitar player has an orchestra in his hands.

—JEFF BUCKLEY

I was the hot-shot guitarist on the block—I thought I was it. I went across the street and saw him. Hendrix knew who I was, and that day, in front of my eyes, he burned me to death. I didn't even get my guitar out. H-bombs were going off, guided missiles were flying—I can't tell you the sounds he was getting out of his instrument. . . . How he did this, I wish I understood. He just got right up in my face with that axe, and I didn't even want to pick up a guitar for the next year.

—MIKE BLOOMFIELD (1943–1981), on his
first time seeing newcomer Jimi Hendrix play

The music I might hear I can't get on the guitar. It's a thing of just laying around daydreaming or something. You're hearing all this music, and you just can't get it on the guitar. As a matter of fact, if you pick up your guitar and just try to play, it spoils the whole thing. I can't play the guitar that well to get all this music together.

—JIMI HENDRIX (1942–1970)

I play so simply that I find it astounding that anyone rates me as a guitarist at all.

—PETE TOWNSHEND, 1968

I became a drummer because it was the only thing I could do. But whenever I hear another drummer I know I'm no good.

—RINGO STARR

I realized that Ringo was an excellent drummer for what was required. He's not a "technical" drummer. . . . But he's a good solid rock drummer with a super steady beat and he knows how to get the right sound out of his drums. Above all, he does have an individual sound. You can tell Ringo's drums from anyone else's, and that character was a definite asset to the Beatles' early recordings.

—GEORGE MARTIN, conductor who
arranged the classical instrumentation on many
Beatles recordings

Charlotte [Caffey] says some of my chord progressions are really weird, and that if I knew anything about music they wouldn't exist. So that's good.

—JANE WEIDLIN, of the Go-Go's, 1995

Maybe if I worked on my guitar playing we'd attract a better class of people.

—JOE PERRY, of Aerosmith, 1979

> By the time I started recording, they would say to me, "Do you read music?" And I'd say, "Not enough to hurt my pickin'."
>
> —ROY ORBISON (1936–1988)

I don't necessarily look at myself as self-taught. I would sit down and listen to something and if I couldn't find it on the [guitar] neck yet, I would learn to find it singing the best I could. Trying to find the sound with my lips and my mouth, doing some bastardized version of scat singing. Then I would learn to make the sound with my fingers that I was making with my mouth.

—STEVIE RAY VAUGHN (1954–1990)

You play yourself into a corner, and then by accident you try something and it really works. You're looking at the guitar, thinking, "Whose hands are those?"

—STEPHEN STILLS, 1995

[The rest of the band will] follow me down any dark alley. Sometimes there's a light at the end of the alley, and sometimes there's a black hole. The point is, you don't get an adventure in music unless you're willing to take chances. —JERRY GARCIA (1942–1995), of the Grateful Dead, on his lead guitar experimentation

When you play from your heart, all of a sudden there's no gravity. You don't feel the weight of the world, of bills, of anything. That's why people love it. Your so-called insurmountable problems disappear, and instead of problems you get possibilities.
—CARLOS SANTANA, 1995

The only place where I've never felt guilty or shameful is when I've been playing [piano]. It's the only place where I've felt in touch with my sexuality and my spirituality and my emotions, and never, ever, anywhere else. —TORI AMOS, 1994

What I'm trying to do [when I play guitar] is find that clarity, when I can let go of whatever it would be, ego or self-consciousness. Since I can't read music, I find I do best when I just listen to where I'm trying to go with it and where it can go. And try not to rush it. . . . When I've played from my mind I get in trouble.
—STEVIE RAY VAUGHN (1954–1990)

I like creative guitar. I don't especially dig like, a rock 'n' roll solo or a blues solo, where guitarists regularly play. Ya know? I like creative things. —BOB MARLEY (1945–1981), 1975

I want the idea and the sound of the idea to intoxicate—not the voltage. Otherwise it's a mindless thrusting that brings nothing but repulsion. —JEFF BUCKLEY

Acoustic guitar is *the* instrument because it can't fool you, you can't make tricks with the acoustic. If you keep the acoustic up, it'll help the electric guitar-playing. Otherwise you can get into that Fastest Guitar in the West syndrome, which is, for rock 'n' roll, absolutely a dead-end street. That's rock music, but it ain't rock 'n' roll.
—KEITH RICHARDS, 1989

Anybody who takes a 20-minute guitar solo should be shot, and I mean that. If it takes you 20 minutes to say something, then don't bother. —ROBERT CRAY, 1987

Drum solos are fucking boring. Any kind of solo is. It detracts from the group identity. —KEITH MOON (1946–1978), of the Who, 1971

I'm philosophically opposed to the notion of the "guitar hero." I'm more into the song hero. —JOHN FLANSBURGH, of They Might Be Giants

You've got to hate that whole guitar-as-penis thing. . . . The more solos you do, the more of a man you are. Because that's the implication. It's also complete bullshit.

—PETER BUCK, of R.E.M., 1991

When we get together and jam, it's a big hard-on.
—SCOTT WEILAND, of Stone Temple Pilots, 1995

When the band [is] really cooking, it tend[s] to make one transcend oneself. —DAVID BYRNE, of Talking Heads, 1983

The guitar for me has always been a gun. And the only thing you could do with a machine gun in the '60s was break it across your legs, and that's what I did. I suppose that I do sometimes sit down with an acoustic guitar and try to use the guitar as an instrument of love and communication. But even the way I play acoustic is very aggressively rhythmic. My best work is rhythmic and machine-gunny.

—PETE TOWNSHEND, 1994

I really learned to play as a member of the Doors. I just tried to sound like myself—I consciously avoided copying Chuck Berry or B. B. King because that's what everyone was doing. I tried to come up with the right part for the song and play something that would complement Jim's singing. It must have worked. I think we came up with a pretty good body of work.

—ROBBY KRIEGER, of the Doors, 1994

When you're young, your attitude is "Hey, we'll pay *you* to let us play!" You'd do it for nothing! Between you and I, we would still do it for nothing! If it was all to stop tomorrow, we'd be playing in bars. Because this is what we do, record deals or not, hits or not, we'd play.

—JIM KERR, of Simple Minds, 1991

songwriting: killing me softly

think the best I'm hoping for is just a real good song. —JAMES TAYLOR

I remember someone telling me: "You write great melodies, and you know great chords, but you should cut writing the lyrics shit out. Don't even think about it." And they were serious!
—STEVIE WONDER, 1995

People . . . didn't think of me as a songwriter, so when I started coming up with songs, they'd look at me like: "Who really wrote that?" I don't know what they must have thought—that I had someone back in the garage who was writing them for me?
—MICHAEL JACKSON

I don't write or read music at all. I have to describe things to people if I'm working with a writer or arranger; I have to communicate by humming the lines, which can get very tedious.
—ELVIS COSTELLO, 1983

We don't always know what we're doing. We often just get excited, put something down, and say, "Oh, neat."
—TINA WEYMOUTH, of Talking Heads

As I accidentally tripped over ideas, I found that although I was definitely flailing, I was also discovering something new and inventing something. —ROBBIE ROBERTSON, of the Band

My songs are really personal but a lot of the time I shroud the meanings on purpose. I write in metaphors and symbolism and double meanings and get them all tangled up, so you have to be at least into it or clever enough to untangle it.

—KAT BJELLAND, of Babes in Toyland, 1994

See, I believe it's no good to talk about your songs; it's wrong. You should leave your songs alone and let them say what they say; let people take what they want from them. All I try to do in the songs is write about the world that I'm in, and I try to do it honestly. But it's no good to explain. If they were meant to be explained then they wouldn't be written.

—PAUL SIMON, 1975

Sometimes I'm not sure what a lot of our songs are about.

—JIM KERR, of Simple Minds

Our music isn't about telling people how they should act or it isn't, like, preaching. We're not politicians. We're musicians, and sometimes we even have a hard time even believing *that*. Most of the stuff is just about personal stuff. The solutions I find for *myself*. . . when I write. I sometimes look at it later on and I go, "God, I was totally being a dork."

—BILLIE JOE ARMSTRONG,
of Green Day, 1996

I knew I wanted to write literature in the pop arena, and in a way I was really punished for it. Even by John Lennon. He told me that I was a product of my own over-education—and remember, I only have a twelfth-grade education.

—JONI MITCHELL, 1991

What I learned from [Bob] Dylan is to go straight for the heart in your music. I think people often get caught up too much in the specifics of a song and try to intellectualize it, when the important thing is just to strike an emotion. Sometimes just a breath in a song can make you weep.

—P. J. HARVEY, 1995

God has blessed me with all these songs. Some of them are better than others . . . but none of them are really bad. What did I do to deserve them? I can't answer that question. I can't understand blessings, but I recognize them, I cherish them.

—STEVIE WONDER, 1995

I wake up from dreams and go, "Wow, put this down on paper." The whole thing is strange. You hear the words, everything is right there in front of your face. And you say to yourself, "I'm sorry, I just didn't write this. It's there already." That's why I hate to take credit for the songs I've written. I feel that somewhere, someplace, it's been done and I'm just a courier bringing it into the world. I really believe that. —MICHAEL JACKSON, 1983

When you write a song that sounds really good . . . you think, surely it must be someone else's. —PETE SHELLEY, of the Buzzcocks

To get an idea for a song and to make it work is still the hardest thing and most important thing I do. Every time I write a song that I am happy with there is a part of me saying that I may never write another one. —LYLE LOVETT, 1995

I've tried to use songs to seduce, to make people long for me, to keep people away, to threaten people, to define my territory, to talk about my fears. But also to turn people toward God, and to give people hope who haven't got any hope, especially people who might feel inadequate because of the way they look. . . . So some of the things I've used songs for are very, very good, and some of them are very selfish. —PETE TOWNSHEND, 1989

I want to create songs that include a lot of ordinary people, [songs] that raise their self-esteem. —JOHN MELLENCAMP, 1987

From now on, I want to write from inside me, and to do that I'm going to have to get back to writing like I used to when I was ten—

having everything come out naturally. The way I like to write is for it to come out the way I talk.

—BOB DYLAN

The songs about small bits of life. The songs that point out something that exists in human nature. Those are the kind of things I enjoy writing about. Those are the kinds of songs that move me.

—LYLE LOVETT, 1992

I think for every situation there's a song.

—BJÖRK

There's really only one song in the whole wide world, and Adam and Eve hummed it to each other, and everything else is a variation on it in one form or another, you know?

—KEITH RICHARDS, 1989

I try not to repeat myself. It's the hardest thing in the world to do—there are only so many notes one human being can master.

—PRINCE

I used to try to make stuff that I thought people would want to hear, and my friends'd say, "No, man, tell them that shit about the neighborhood." I would think nobody would want to hear that, that's depressing. And they would say, "People want to hear that; everybody don't live like you, they don't see what you see, you've got to wake people up."

—ICE-T, 1992

I definitely don't try to write songs that someone's definitely going to relate to.

—BILLIE JOE ARMSTRONG,
of Green Day, 1995

I didn't realize until I started writing [songs] that I actually had things I wanted to say. It wasn't until the records had come out and we got on tour and people came up and said, "Oh, yeah, I really relate to that." I thought, "How strange that people think the way I do."

—RAY DAVIES, of the Kinks, 1995

Each of my songs has a specific audience. It really is just a way to express feeling, like writing somebody a letter. But somehow I feel that if you write a song for somebody, they feel it more. I could be wrong. Maybe it's that the emotional impact for me is greater. It could be a selfish thing, because I feel that I've retained something from the relationship.　　　　　—LYLE LOVETT, 1992

Sometimes I think I should go back to being a waitress; maybe I would enjoy life more. But if I led a perfectly existing life, where I didn't try the universe or dare anybody or take any risks, I would never have written all these songs!

　　　　　　　　　—STEVIE NICKS, 1989

I always needed a song to get by. There's a lot of singers who don't need songs to get by. A lot of 'em are tall, good-lookin', you know? They don't need to say anything in order to grab people. Me, I had to make it on something other than my looks or my voice.

　　　　　　　　　—BOB DYLAN, 1987

Someone said my songwriting was like cheap home therapy, but I don't know, it's more like a journal.

　　　　　　　　　—BILLIE JOE ARMSTRONG, of Green Day

I do tend to work things out in my songs and usually something I've been hiding comes out—a certain feeling—and it's freeing, it's liberating. And I really can't walk around and be crippled for the rest of my life.　　　　　　—TORI AMOS

I only compose songs if I'm in an emotional state, if I'm experiencing extreme happiness, extreme sadness or grief. Then I compose because I have to fix myself. I compose to heal myself from damage.

　　　　　　　　　—ERIC CLAPTON, 1992

All my songs are therapy. I'm giving therapy to myself.

　　　　　　　　　—SEAL

With writing, you have to plumb into the subconscious, and there's a lot of scary things down there—like a bad dream sometimes. If

109

you can extricate yourself from it and face up to it, you come back with a lot of self-knowledge, which then gives you a greater human knowledge, and that helps. So in a way, the writing process is fantastic psychotherapy—if you can survive—but it's tricky.

—JONI MITCHELL, 1992

I've written my best things when I'm upset. What's the point of sitting down and notating your happiness?

—MADONNA

If you're pissed off, or you just want to tidy out your brain, it's good if you talk to somebody. But sometimes it's the same goodness if you talk out loud to yourself; it seems to sort things into neat little piles. [My] songs are just me tidying my brain.

—SINÉAD O'CONNOR, 1990

I use my songs as a way to awaken myself. It's like sticking a needle in your leg after it has gone to sleep.

—BONO

What I look for in music and what I want to produce is just . . . works that are moving and unsettling—an emotional assault. I don't want to write a song that just washes over my head and makes me feel nothing.

—P. J. HARVEY, 1995

What I try to do [when I write songs], which is a very American thing I guess, is to dig in and try to find the truth in an idea.

—BOB SEGER, 1983

The world don't need any more songs. If nobody wrote any songs from this day on, the world ain't gonna suffer it.

—BOB DYLAN, 1991

We feel a responsibility as songwriters not to lead the young kids into drugs, like we were led in the '60s. Not to clobber them with political stuff, and not to lead them into anarchy or stupid things like devil worship. All we want to do is give people an uplifting entertainment experience. Because life is tough. People at large need us. You need art. You need to look at something beautiful each day.

—TERRY BOZZIO, of Missing Persons, 1983

We never completely do a song just to please ourselves. We bring everybody we can into the studio, even the receptionist, so that we can get their opinions. We put about 30 percent of what we consider to be art into our records and about 70 percent of it is writing for the public. . . . And we don't dwell too much on deep stories, because today people want to hear songs about love. Each song in the Top 20 is about love. Every album in the Top 10 is based on love.

—BARRY GIBB, of the Bee Gees, 1979

You know, I'm starting to feel pretty good. I know I've written some classic songs that someday are going to be elevator music, and that makes me feel pretty good.

—CHRISTOPHER CROSS, 1983

I refuse to slap some stupid words on the stupid paper just so we have a stupid song finished.

—SUZANNE VEGA

> **I don't give a hang if I never make another record that has any appeal to it whatsoever.**
> —DAVID BOWIE, 1983

I just do what I feel like doing. I just write songs for myself, I don't do them for anybody else and I don't have a great big message to give anybody.

—SINÉAD O'CONNOR, 1988

You make records for other people, not for yourself. That's what it's about. I'm making it for the market place. After I write it, I don't think about it.

—VAN MORRISON

I've never stressed it enough that I write from my own point of view. I'm not writing for anybody else. What people identify with in the songs is their business. That's what use they make of the songs, the same way they make use of something they've read in a book or see in a film. I don't make any demands on the audience in terms of them seeing me as a spokesperson or a champion. I don't cast myself in any roles like those. I'm just an individual.

—ELVIS COSTELLO, 1983

Early on, I accepted that once a song is pressed and it goes out to people, it's as much theirs as it is mine. Anything anyone wants to see in them is fine.   —MICHAEL STIPE, of R.E.M.

I didn't realize people took songs so seriously, and it made me wonder whether I ought to consider the consequences [of what I write].

—JIM MORRISON (1943–1971), 1969

My stuff is definitely up for discussion. When you're listening to an Ice-T album you're listening to me in the middle of a park yelling out my attitudes, my ideas. You can agree or disagree. But you should never think everything I'm thinking. 'Cause then only one of us is thinking.

—ICE-T, 1991

What I'm trying to do [when I write songs] is reduce words and images and sounds down to the bone.

—BRYAN FERRY, of Roxy Music, 1985

When I get an idea [for a song] it tickles.

—CHRIS ISAAK, 1995

When I write tunes, they're more about the foreplay than the intercourse, because as a true female, I guess that's what I'm more interested in. I'd rather play with my imagination and flirt more with my head.   —BJÖRK, 1994

My songs are more about love than they are about sex. I don't consider myself a great poet, or interpreter à la Moses. I just know I'm here to say what's on my mind, and I'm in a position where I can do that. It would be foolish for me to make up stories about going to Paris, knocking off the queen and things of that nature.

—PRINCE

Beside the "confessional" assumption, people assume that everything I write is autobiographical. If I sing in first person, they think it's all about me.... Certainly, most of the song is eyewitness accounting, but many of the characters I write about—even if their tone is entirely first person—have nothing to do with my own life in the intimate sense. It's more like dramatic recitation or theatrical soliloquy.

—JONI MITCHELL, 1988

When you get very autobiographical [in songwriting], it's suddenly too insular, and the reference points are not as easily understood. I try to take it to one ring outside of that, keeping the world in mind. I try to link up universal ideas with my own experience.

—BILLY CORGAN, of the Smashing Pumpkins, 1995

I've always felt that a lot of my songs deal with spying on myself.

—CARLY SIMON, 1981

A large amount of stuff I was doing [musically] was self-definition, exercises in trying different aspects of myself on for size—sometimes fanciful, sometimes serious, sometimes happenstantial.

—JAMES TAYLOR, 1981

Eating yourself away, going inside yourself and internalizing things are not very healthy things to do. You have to get out and find some perspective—go and do some gardening, watch some telly. When I come back to the songs, I see them clearly.

—P. J. HARVEY, on the introspection of songwriting, 1995

I'm not interested in revealing myself in songs.

—TANYA DONELLY, of Belly

I'm not really worried about exposing too much of myself in the songs, because I change a lot and I change really fast. My point of view changes every few months, so if I expose a lot of myself at one time it won't matter because I'm not gonna feel the same way later.

—JULIANA HATFIELD

I don't sit down to write goofy cornball lyrics. Nobody wants to be thought of as just some goofball. But I am a big fan of stories that are, on the surface, harmless and cute or whatever, but have a certain eeriness and evilness and nastiness to them. It's kind of like Roald Dahl: if you read *Charlie and the Chocolate Factory*... Dahl has some twisted weird stuff going on.

—LES CLAYPOOL, of Primus, 1995

Not that you can't write about a serious subject—everything can't be a goof—but I think you just get it a little easier if you don't get all puffed up. —TOM PETTY, 1990

The songs make certain demands. And they take on their own personalities. It's like I'm creating monsters, like making The Thing! They follow me around. I have some of them that hang out for years. —TORI AMOS, 1992

> **A song has a real body. It moves and changes and you [can] adopt it and live in it for a while.**
> —KRISTIN HERSH, of Throwing Muses, 1994

I usually rewrite songs for a long time, sometimes for years. I keep trying to uncover what it is I am trying to say. I know that if I stop too soon I'll end up with slogans.

—LEONARD COHEN, 1995

Yes, I think I have something important to say. I never thought I'd really have to worry about that. But you do, when you've made years of landmark records in the past. Can you make another one? . . . You're constantly coming up with a new way of looking at the world that is different from the way you looked at it five years ago. And the world is changing. So it's continually rejuvenating, the creative process. —RAY DAVIES, of the Kinks, 1995

I don't know what real childbirth is like, but writing songs seems as close as I'm going to come. —BILLY JOEL

Without the word dream, or the concept dream, and without the word blue and the emotions, I would have been really limited in the things I've written and performed.

—ROY ORBISON (1936–1988)

The idea that I am a "shocking" artist is hysterical. It is a way more accurate reflection of the country's morality, the puritan upbringing. . . . If you can't hear beyond the "fucks," you shouldn't be listening to [my music] because the "fucks" have an absolute meaning in the sentences. It isn't just there to shock. It is telling a story.

—LIZ PHAIR, 1995

We're not trying to shock anybody. We're trying to write songs that we like. We're constantly described as being sleazy and gross and words like that, and I don't think any of our songs are [like that] at all. They may be too sexual for some people who are repressed, but there's nothing unsavory about them.

—LUX INTERIOR, of the Cramps, 1995

I'm like a fisherman. I get my poetry from Senegal and go across the Atlantic. And when I see this country, I bring back those fish to Senegal.

—YOUSSOU N'DOUR, on his
cross-cultural songs

The songs that come out depend on what I've had to eat or drink and what's on my ever-wandering mind. Sometimes you're surprised by yourself.

—SYD STRAW, 1995

I see songwriting as having to do with experience, and the more you've experienced, the better it is. But it has to be tempered, and you just must let your imagination run. You can't just experience something and leave it at that. You've got to try and embroider, like any kind of writing. And that's the fun part of it.

—MICK JAGGER, 1994

Those first few songs I wrote, I was taking notes at a fantastic rock concert going on in my head.

—JIM MORRISON (1943–1971), 1969

In the early days John [Lennon] and I used to steal, man. You know that quote: A bad artist borrows from others, a good artist steals. We used to call it nicking. "I Saw Her Standing There" is "Talking About You" by Chuck Berry. "Come Together" is a complete nick of Chuck Berry, slowed down.　　—PAUL McCARTNEY, 1990

When I started writing all those songs and everyone started calling me a genius—genius this and genius that . . . I knew it was bull, because I still hadn't written what I wanted to. I had written "Blowin' in the Wind," but I wasn't satisfied with that. I was never satisfied with "Blowin' in the Wind." I wrote that in ten minutes. "Blowin' in the Wind" was a lucky classic song. No more, no less than "Your Cheatin' Heart." But it was one-dimensional.
　　　　　　　　　　　　　　　　—BOB DYLAN, 1986

I don't know whether I have the ability to come up with more. I have to do a lot of hard work before I can get anywhere near those stages of consistent, total brilliance.
　　　　　　　　　　—JIMMY PAGE, of Led Zeppelin, on what
　　　　　　　　　　comes after "Stairway to Heaven"

How could you possibly top "The End"? What's left once you've fucked your mother and killed your father?
　　　　　　　　　　—ROBBY KRIEGER, of the Doors; while they
　　　　　　　　　　were in the recording studio working on "The
　　　　　　　　　　End," an acid-tripping Jim Morrison began
　　　　　　　　　　chanting "fuck the mother, kill the father"; they
　　　　　　　　　　used it on the song; 1994

When we were turning out those Police albums I felt very close to the pulse. . . . I knew when we were writing hits. "This is a hit, that's not a hit, this is a hit." Now I don't know anymore. I don't really feel I have my finger on the pulse anymore. I think I go a little bit deeper, so it takes longer. . . . Ideas don't come that readily. . . . So then you have to go for quality, you have to go with saying more with less.　　　　　—STING, 1991

Deep down we are songwriters first and foremost. We can write a beautiful ballad and then turn around and write . . .
　　　　　　　　　　—MAURICE GIBB
. . . a load of crap!　　　　—BARRY GIBB, of the Bee Gees, 1979

If I had written "I Love You Just the Way You Are," I probably would have added "You Little Shit"—I throw in something to blow it out of the water every time. . . . Billy Joel has a track record of reinventing himself, and that's very difficult. It's a talent to have. I have a track record too, which includes almost no hits.

—RANDY NEWMAN, 1995

Oh, well, we were new at writing songs and new at playing our instruments, so we couldn't write anything too complicated, really. It was nothing intentional. We decided to sing about something that we found amusing.

—JOHNNY RAMONE, on the simplicity of
the Ramones' songs, 1979

In Beatles days we used to throw saucy little things in, but most of it was stuff the critics made up. . . . That's how the times were anyway, all colored by acid and pot. Mainly those songs were very straightforward, but our image was so bizarre.

—PAUL McCARTNEY, on the hidden
messages in the Beatles' songs on
Sgt. Pepper's, 1987

I came up with the phrase "bad to the bone," then it took me several months to write all the lyrics. I wanted them to be like an old Muddy Waters or Bo Diddley song—exotic, tough, mythic lyrics. . . . I actually wrote "Bad to the Bone" for [Muddy] to sing, because I just couldn't hear myself doing it. We tried to peddle it to Muddy, but he declined. . . . I literally could not peddle it to anyone so I recorded it myself. And it became the song I'm best-known for.

—GEORGE THOROGOOD

["We Will Rock You"] was a response to a particular phase in our career—when the audience was becoming a bigger part of the show than we were. They would sing all the songs. Sometimes, they'd be so vociferous that we'd have to stop the show and let them sing to us. So both Freddie [Mercury] and I thought it would be an interesting experiment to write songs with audience participation specifically in mind—everyone can stamp and clap and sing a simple motif. . . . It's amazing to go to sports events and hear people do it. It's very gratifying to find that it has become part of folklore. I'll die happy because of that.

—BRIAN MAY, of Queen

Simplicity is the key to ["Smoke on the Water's"] endurance. And it is simple—you can still hear people playing it at music stores. I never had the courage to write until I heard "I Can't Explain" and "My Generation" [by the Who]. Those riffs were so straightforward that I thought, "All right, if Pete Townshend can get away with that, then I can, too!"

—RITCHIE BLACKMORE, of Deep Purple

I wrote a lot of songs in high school. They were all derivative, pretentious, and goofy; pretty much sound like the things I'm doing now.

—CHRIS ISAAK, 1995

We would try to play other people's songs, but we just couldn't play them. We played them so badly, we decided to write our own songs.

—BONO, on the early days of U2

We aren't singing about high-rise flats in London. We are singing about cigarettes and alcohol and following your dreams and everyday life, and that means as much to people in Denver as people in London.

—NOEL GALLAGHER, of Oasis, on why the British band has had such success in the United States, 1995

We would leave the computer on for days and go in at separate times or together and hash out an arrangement. Doing a drum or vocal line in your underwear a little hung over at 10 A.M. is better than having an engineer shoving a mike down your throat.

—LIESEGANG, of Filter, on why his band writes songs at home instead of in a studio, 1995

Freddie [Mercury] used to come into the studio armed with sheets and sheets of paper, with notes scribbled all over them in his own particular fashion. It wasn't standard musical notation at all—it looked like buses zooming all over his bits of paper.

—BRIAN MAY, of Queen

Fame &
Fortune
and the
Biz

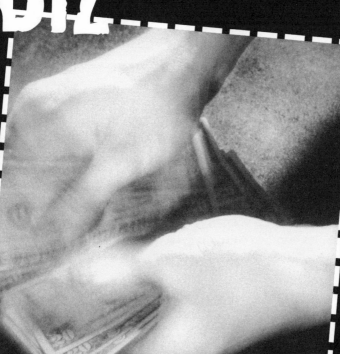

so ya wanna be a rock 'n' roll star

Stardom and fame is bullshit that sucks you in and if you're not fortunate you can get so sucked in that you start believing it.

—GEORGE HARRISON, 1992

You could be stuck with a band because it's successful. Soft chairs and nice cars are not really what it's about.

—RIC OCASEK, of the Cars, 1991

The danger of fame is in forgetting or being distracted.

—BRUCE SPRINGSTEEN

Fame is what everyone wants in some form or another.

—PAUL McCARTNEY

I won't be happy until I'm as famous as God.

—MADONNA

As long as I can remember, since I was a little kid, I wanted to be famous. It was the mythological means of escape. My myth was rock-god-dom. I saw that as a means to become one who has no pain.

—BILLY CORGAN, of the Smashing Pumpkins

When we started the band, we wanted to be rich and famous. *Famous.* That was a requirement. I mean, what a stupid thing to want. We actually wanted fame, fortune and probably all to live in one house with a fire pole in the middle.

—ANDY PARTRIDGE, of XTC, 1989

121

Madame Tussaud's will have my statue. I just hope they don't make me look like James Brown.   —LITTLE RICHARD

Barbara Walters knows who I am? Shit! I must be famous.

      —COURTNEY LOVE, of Hole, 1995

I mean, we used to eat Mrs. Paul's frozen fish sticks. Now we eat these little chilled shrimp. Same thing.

      —JIM SONEFELD, of Hootie & the
      Blowfish, 1995

I knew [the Beatles would] be bigger than Elvis. I knew they'd be the biggest theatrical attraction in the world.

      —BRIAN EPSTEIN (1934–1967),
      the Beatles' manager

I'm
an instant star;
just add water
and stir.
—DAVID BOWIE

I liken our success to Jiffy Pop popcorn. All of a sudden there's just a rise to fame. Poof. And we're transformed into . . . something else.

      —EDIE BRICKEL, 1987

I don't know what it is. I just fell into it really. My daddy and I were laughing about it the other day. He looked at me and said, "What happened, El? The last thing I can remember is I was working in a can factory, and you were driving a truck." We all feel the same way about it still. It just . . . caught us up.

      —ELVIS PRESLEY (1935–1977), on his
      overnight success, 1956

Believe me, all of this has fallen in my lap. I was never good at getting jobs or girls or anything. . . . I didn't know that you could get paid for playing. —BECK

You can't imagine what it was like having a hit record behind you at the age of 16. One month [Art Garfunkel] and I were watching *American Bandstand* on the television, and the next month we were on the show. It was an incredible thing to have happen to you in your adolescence. I had picked up the guitar because I wanted to be like Elvis Presley, and there I was!
—PAUL SIMON, 1975

You see, success like we have now was just a very distant dream in 1971. . . . And now we can't really accept what we've done and where we are when we read magazines saying, "The Bee Gees are hot." But sooner or later these bubbles burst anyway, and I would like for the Bee Gees to stop before we wane. . . . All the bubbles have a way of bursting or being deflated in the end.
—BARRY GIBB, of the Bee Gees, 1979

When you're a rock star, you're allowed to be a petulant child and many other things you're supposed to grow out of.
—STING, 1983

Five years ago I would get annoyed when my [welfare] check arrived a day late. The next thing I know, I'm getting pissed off if my limo didn't turn up. —SEAL, 1994

It's wearing. You're on all the time. . . . I'd rather be having one day where I don't have to think about me. With all this attention, you become a child. It's awful to be at the center of attention. You can't talk about anything apart from your own experience, your own dopey life. —MICK JAGGER, 1994

Rock star means, like, a rich asshole. That's a 1980s thing. No matter what anyone says, I'm too deeply rooted to just turn asshole overnight. —MIKE DIRNT, of Green Day

If I'm smart enough to get in the position of popularity, and I don't take that popularity and that wisdom and that wealth I've accumulated to do anything but to feed myself O. J.-style, who the fuck needs me on the planet? —PERRY FARRELL, 1997

One of the challenges and one of the drawbacks of becoming famous is that you become aware of the fact that everybody's going to hear what you're singing, so you become a little bit more cagey. You've got to overcome that, you've got to say what you've got to say.
—DOLORES O'RIORDAN, of the
Cranberries, 1995

If reaching a larger market means that you have to sound like Christopher Cross, then I'd rather stay where I am.
—ELVIS COSTELLO, 1983

As soon as you get to a certain point, it's no longer hip to dig you.
—KRIS KRISTOFFERSON

Some part of me is feeling that maybe I've done something wrong if I'm this popular. —SUZANNE VEGA, 1987

The majority of pop stars are complete idiots in every respect.
—SADE

Achievement is for the senators and scholars. At one time I had ambitions, but I had them removed by a doctor in Buffalo.
—TOM WAITS

I didn't have the drive to be a star. I just wanted to make a nice living and be on a bill with Jackson Browne.
—BONNIE RAITT

Without [U2], I think I wouldn't know where I'd be as a person—I think I'd make a pretty shitty bank manager.
—BONO

[The Eagles] tried to maintain that underdog frame of mind.
—GLENN FREY

But it was hard to be an underdog when you're selling 12 million records.
—DON HENLEY, 1990

Our music was in this world of fame and glam and lights. We all realized, "Wow, we have taken something that is pure to us, and somebody bought it and exploited it, and now we're able to make a living."
—ED KOWALCZYK, of Live, 1996

1978. Boom! I made it. Money comes in. Tons of money. . . . Doing drugs and coke and all kinds of drinking. Thinking I'm some kind of god.
—RICK JAMES

Once money spoil you, boy, you ain't got no friends. You friends is your money—that mean that all the people we have around here, them like you because you have money—and then when your money done, you're finished. . . . Money done, you ain't got no woman, neither!
—BOB MARLEY (1945–1981), 1975

A million dollars ain't nothin' now. Once you get that million, you want more millions. Some of the happiest people are poor people. . . . I love money, but I'm not happy right now. I can be happy, at times. I'm happy onstage. That's the only place I'm happy.
—BOBBY BROWN, 1989

Security is the only thing I want. Money to do nothing with, money to have in case you wanted to do something.
—PAUL McCARTNEY

All I ever wanted to do was sin and make a lot of money as well.
—MICK JAGGER

I read my first article [when I was 12] about [a major 1980s rock star], and he was in a limo doing lines of blow on a mirror, and he had babes under each arm. And that's when I decided I wanted to be a rock star. I wanted to do blow, and I wanted those babes under my arms. I didn't know what blow was, and I didn't know what sex was, but it looked impressive to me because it was written in the magazine. —LAYNE STALEY, of Alice in Chains, 1996

Money and girls were the two big motivations—that's what it was for everybody. Then you become a serious artist and set out to change the world. —DON HENLEY, on why he wanted to become a rock star

I want to be extremely successful. But success for me, I think, means something a bit different from what it means maybe for U2. I'd like to be successful in the fact that I'd like to be a prolific, ongoing writer that is successful in terms of building people's respect. I am not all that interested in making loads of money or having loads of record sales. I am more concerned with the matter of respect. —P. J. HARVEY, 1995

There were moments when it was very confusing, because I realized that I was a rich man, but I felt like a poor man inside. —BRUCE SPRINGSTEEN, 1984

The bigger you get, the less you can work—which is never a good thing for a musician. —KEITH RICHARDS, 1989

I often find that success is perceived much more by people outside than by the people who're involved in it. The people who're involved in it are usually so bloody busy that they don't have time to think about it at all. —MARK KNOPFLER, of Dire Straits, 1983

Being noticed can be a burden. Jesus got himself crucified because he got himself noticed. So I disappear a lot. —BOB DYLAN

I'm not doing it for the fame. I hate attention. I always want to be back of the class, but for some reason people seem to pull me out front. —BJÖRK, 1995

There are times when [all the attention] is fun and it is a pageant, but there are times when it is so oppressive that you feel like you are the least powerful person in the situation. Those are the times when it feels that none of the artistry matters . . . that everything is simply a strategy to sell records, and that's when it becomes overwhelming. —LIZ PHAIR, 1995

The mistake [celebrities] make is they confuse that thing that's been created by them and by the media for reality. Then they sit inside that thing and they wonder why everything's fucked up.
—STING, 1991

Being a celebrity is not so great a gig. . . . You end up disappointing the people who thought you were what you never said you were.
—JAMES TAYLOR, 1981

The bigger we got, the more unreality we had to face. . . . It happened bit by bit, gradually until this complete craziness is surrounding you, and you're doing exactly what you don't want to do with people you can't stand—the people you hated when you were 10.
—JOHN LENNON (1940–1980)

You always hear about famous actors and big rock people bitchin' endlessly about payin' taxes and signin' autographs. Well, I think you got a responsibility not to be that way. . . . Hell, I can rent a car now, I can go wherever I want on this earth. I send all my kids to college on just a few songs. . . . I do feel like a shithead signin' autographs; they always ask you when you're hurryin' to catch a plane carryin' three bags and a guitar. But if you don't sign, you feel like more of a shithead. —KRIS KRISTOFFERSON

The legend part is easy. It's the living that's hard.
—KEITH RICHARDS

I may be a living legend, but that sure don't help when I've got to change a tire. —ROY ORBISON (1936–1988)

I've become completely well adjusted to being a cult figure. —LOU REED, 1989

The thing most people don't understand about show business's so-called "personalities" is that our lives are often just as normal as theirs, and if "normal" means being screwed-up, then, yes, I am normal and screwed-up. I try to maintain a certain dignity about it. That's all I can do. —MARVIN GAYE (1939–1984)

I think that maybe fame scares away a lot of friendships, because people just assume that you're getting what you need. When you walk into a performance situation or a record-company office, people really like you, they pay a lot of attention to you. But then, your normal life is the same as anybody's—just as lonely. You can't get anyone on the phone, and you can't get a date. —RICKI LEE JONES, 1979

From being in the public eye, people perceive you differently. They all "yes" you to death when you need friends to tell you "no" sometimes. The hardest thing to find out is who your friends are. I think that in this position, people are looking at what you are and not who you are. —TICO, of Bon Jovi

When you're a kid and you see a group like the Beatles on TV, you say, "I wanna be that." But when you're there, everything's exactly the same, nothing changes. You think, "Ah, a Number One album," like the fucking skies are gonna open up or something—and nothing happens. —JAMES HONEYMAN-SCOTT (d. 1982), of the Pretenders, 1980

Even though I have fame, I have money, I have a wonderful family, I feel very unhappy, because it's always the records that have driven me. It becomes a way of life. . . . Unless you see it go up the charts, you've failed. I was lucky enough to have it all those years; perhaps it'll never come back. Perhaps I don't have that creative spark anymore. Perhaps I'm not hungry enough. I could be bigger. I could be richer. —NEIL SEDAKA

I'm sick of not selling records. I want to draw more people to the shows, make something happen. If the new album isn't a hit, I'm gonna kill myself. —JOEY RAMONE, of the Ramones, 1979

I'm glad we will never be big enough to be in the Rock 'n' Roll Hall of Fame. That's what hell is all about, to be part of an institutionalized legacy machine. Legacy is in the eyes of the beholder. We obviously survived. I suppose the legacy is that a band can stay together for a long time without hit records.

—DANNY ELFMAN, of Oingo Boingo, 1995

We expect celebrities to be superhuman.
But think about it—the thing that drives people to become celebrities is this need for overwhelming love. And when many people get the fame they crave, they don't feel they deserve it. And so they screw up.

—BOY GEORGE, 1995

I've seen a lot of high-flying people hit the big time and then wonder why the fuck they don't feel special. Everybody's calling them special. That's one of the things that I think makes stars tend to take drugs, drink too much. —JAMES TAYLOR, 1981

I got into this business because I love music, not because I saw myself as a big rock star. I mean, look at what happens to rock stars.

—JOAN OSBORNE, 1995

After I got my first gold record, my friend came over and pulled out a couple of lines of blow, and I pulled it off the wall, because that was a dream of mine. If I ever got a gold record, I was going to do my first line of coke on that. I had a great time riding around in limos and eating lobster and getting laid. . . . I had a great time, but I can't physically or mentally live that lifestyle constantly.

—LAYNE STALEY, of Alice in Chains, 1996

I feel pretty lucky to be able to walk around and be somewhat anonymous. If you get removed from reality, you have a lot less source material. But all the really good artists are able to connect with those basic needs and desires of people. It seems like a [famous] person, to get some truth in the writing, has to go down to ground zero where they no longer are themselves.

—JOHN DOE, of X, 1995

You see, in the topsy-turvy Alice in Wonderland world of fame, perceptions are falsified. The exterior becomes so heightened that it is impossible for ordinary mortals to connect the divine ones from everyday activities like urinating, defecating, and vacuuming.

—ANNIE LENNOX, 1995

If the price of fame is that you have to be isolated from the people you write for, then that's too fuckin' high a price to pay.

—BRUCE SPRINGSTEEN

Instead of Messiahs, we always had big rock 'n' roll stars. We like to see who we're worshipping.   —PATTI SMITH

I have sympathy for . . . Kurt Cobain—obviously he was uncomfortable with people coming up to him and saying, "Kurt, you're amazing; you're great," as I think most normal people would be. If you don't have an incredibly needy ego, then it starts to seem kind of surreal at best, and really intrusive at worst. You start to feel that people expect more of you than you could possibly give them. People get the idea that if you're famous you've got some exalted sense of humanity, where the truth is really just the opposite.

—AIMEE MANN, of 'Til Tuesday, 1996

To me, there isn't enough of that [personae] in rock 'n' roll anymore. Now people want celebrities or stars who are just like them. There's a loss of the mystical quality. Where are the Keith Moons, the people who seemed to live in some sort of rock world?

—BLACKIE ONASSIS, of Urge Overkill, 1995

I'm trying to be a public figure and at the same time be average. It's like proclaiming my ordinariness.

—JAMES TAYLOR, 1981

After you've played 100,000-and-some seaters, where do you go? The Empire State Building? Not to knock what Guns [N' Roses] does—that's great—but Guns can't go backward to the point where we all pack up in a van and drive up to a show.

—SLASH

I sometimes wonder if we'll ever wind up back in the bars. The crowds might not always be here. . . . What would it be like playing bars after playing a big tour like this? Probably worse than never making it out in the first place.

—JIM SONEFELD, of Hootie and the
Blowfish, 1995

I felt so relevantly plugged into the times, on that explosion of consciousness that hit popular culture [during the '60s]. I have to say, post-fame was difficult. Because it wasn't just fame, it was superfame of a kind that few have. It was attached to a generation's dreams, and my own personal dreams were mixed up in it, too.

—DONOVAN, on his relative obscurity after
his success in the '60s, 1995

ut, of course I'm a commodity. I know that. And I'm fine with it. Really.

—MICHAEL STIPE, of R.E.M., 1995

I never felt like I ever played a note for the money. I think if I did, people would know, and they'd throw you out of the joint. And you'd deserve to go. —BRUCE SPRINGSTEEN

[The music business is] so much fun, man. I'm like a little kid in a toy store. They keep asking me what toy I wanna play with. And after I spend all day playing with toys, they give me lots of money.

—LIONEL RICHIE, 1983

Somebody said to me, "But the Beatles were antimaterialistic." That's a huge myth. John and I literally used to sit down and say, "Now, let's write a swimming pool."

—PAUL McCARTNEY

That kind of popularity wasn't the reason we originally organized the Stones. We were real serious; we were evangelists at that time. It was a very pure sort of idealistic, adolescent drive that kept us going. The money, we didn't give a damn about the money—at that age, who cares? That wasn't the point. The point was to spread the music. —KEITH RICHARDS

Of course we're doing it for the money as well. . . . We've always done it for the money.

—MICK JAGGER

And while I'm still mostly concerned with making myself happy creatively, I have to confess that the big question mark of how this record will do is always there.   —DAVE NAVARRO, of Red Hot
Chili Peppers

I threatened to quit all the time, but it's, hey, you're in show business until you're in the poor house! You either stay up there, or you begin your decline and the vultures come and pick the last little bit as you go down. As your money diminishes, so does your ability to buy good lawyers to fight the monsters.
—JONI MITCHELL, 1988

As an adult I have been willing to say, "Okay, I'm gonna do the business," because . . . of that business I get to do the art, I get to do the music.   —MELISSA ETHERIDGE, 1995

That's one reason why I like the music business. Because as horrible an empire as it is and as tacky as it is, it's always in transition. They try to control things as much as they can, but they can't—as much as they race around after it. And I like watching that because it's a real microcosm of society. You can't really control it.
—THURSTON MOORE, of Sonic Youth

I thought [rock 'n' roll] was an unassailable outlet for some pure and natural expressions of rebellion. It was one channel you could take without having to kiss ass, you know? And right now it just seems like they're on a big daisy chain, each kissin' each other's asses.
—KEITH RICHARDS

You wonder about people who made a fortune, and you always think they drank it up or they stuck it up their nose. That's not usually what brings on the decline. It's usually the battle to keep your creative child alive while keeping the business shark alive. You have to develop cunning, and shrewdness, and other things which are not well suited to the arts.   —JONI MITCHELL, 1988

To get anywhere in this business you have to be tough and clever. Talent is only half the battle.   —DOLORES O'RIORDAN, of the
Cranberries, 1994

133

I'm way too fucking soft for this whole business. I don't have any shell. There's a contradiction there, because that's why I can write songs that mean something to someone and express some of these things that other people can't. —EDDIE VEDDER, of Pearl Jam, 1995

I wanted to write songs that maybe made 'em think a little bit in between dance steps. That's what I thought my job was. But when you get down to it, it's about how many hit singles you have on the record. —JOHN MELLENCAMP, 1989

> I was a boy in a glass bubble. I couldn't go out:
> I might get hurt. I was a money machine for
> a lot of people.
> —DONNY OSMOND, 1995

We were constantly up against the wall with people saying, "Please us!" It's an invisible thing, but you can feel the wall behind you, and you can hear the whole industry saying, "Give us a surprise, we expect you to outdo yourselves." —BARRY GIBB, of the Bee Gees, 1979

People should realize that [being in this business] is not fun. There are pitfalls to being recognizable. . . . You have no intimacy in your life—nothing. You have a different room every night, and that's a strain in pure brain-function terms. If the brain has too many details to constantly think about . . . you get incredible stress; you get breakdown.

—AIMEE MANN, of 'Til Tuesday, 1996

The music business was not safe, but it was *fun*. It was like falling in love with a woman you know is bad for you, but you love every minute with her, anyway. —LIONEL RICHIE, 1983

I have a great job. I go to work with a beer in my hand. Just a bunch of belligerent drunks running around the world.

—MARC FORD, of the Black Crowes, 1995

We didn't all get into music for a job! We got into it to avoid a job, in truth—and get lots of girls.

—PAUL McCARTNEY, 1987

I wasn't forced into this business, I did it because I enjoyed it and because it was to me as drawing breath and exhaling it. I did it because I was compelled to do it, not by my parents or family, but my own inner life in the world of music.

—MICHAEL JACKSON

I never envisioned what I was doing as part of a career. We just looked at the bands we idolized—like the Yardbirds—and we were blown away by how they could play. All we wanted to do was play like that, to be a great band like that.

—JOE PERRY, of Aerosmith

We weren't out to ruin the music business. There's room for everybody.

—JOHNNY RAMONE,
of the Ramones, 1979

I was young. Being taken out for dinner in a fancy Manhattan restaurant was more impressive than anything the person from the record company actually had to say. I was more involved with the price of the entree: "An $18 plate of vegetables—and I'm getting it for free. Where do I sign?"

—NATALIE MERCHANT, on signing her
first label contract in 1980, 1995

As a young musician, how do you get to be unique, when a record company doesn't want to sign unique people?

—FRANK ZAPPA (1940–1993), 1991

Virgin offered me a deal in 1979, and I turned 'em down . . . offered me a lot of money. I asked Richard Branson [founder of Virgin] to name two songs off my last album, and he couldn't do it. So I told him to fuck off.   —ELVIS COSTELLO

The thing the kids don't understand is that record companies really don't give a shit. They're just looking for the next piece of product to come along. Nobody really cares about whether they have a long and successful career. So you have to plan it and care for it yourself. And like it or not, you have to be a bit of a business man.

—JIMMY BUFFET, 1995

A recording studio isn't much different from a factory. It's just a factory for music. —VAN MORRISON

Just as it is with literature, where Faulkner remains on the library shelves while Jacqueline Susann hits the charts, it's the same with records. Each company must do its best to fill the pulsating needs of mediocrity in order to maximize its potential for success. We might as well be selling hubcaps.

—JERRY WEXLER,
V.P. of Atlantic Records, 1979

[The record companies would] love to get rid of musicians entirely, those bothersome things that talk back and want to do it better.

—KEITH RICHARDS, 1992

What pisses me off is when I've got seven or eight record company fat pig men sitting there telling me what to wear.

—SINÉAD O'CONNOR

You're dealing with mental pygmies in these record companies. Not to cast aspersions on any pygmies in the audience, but these guys do not have musical priorities. Their priority is, "Keep my job, keep my job." —FRANK ZAPPA (1940–1993), 1991

Groups with guitars are on the way out.

—record label Decca's reasoning behind their
cancellation of a 1961 audition of an unsigned
band called the Beatles

The record company aren't nice people; everything they do for you they later take back. They aren't there to be your buddy, it's all business. —DOLORES O'RIORDAN, of the
Cranberries, 1995

All we ever heard about record company people was that they were vampires and criminals and killed Elvis Presley.

—BJÖRK

When I first knew Elvis, he had a million dollars' worth of talent. Now he has a million dollars.

—COLONEL TOM PARKER (1919–1997),
Elvis Presley's manager

Most managers are money men. I guess I have to be one too but I'm not really one at heart. I'd much rather be out on the road with the boys, looking after them. My one dream is seeing the boys in their dressing rooms. No journalists, no fans, no theater people—just the boys.

—BRIAN EPSTEIN (1934–1967),
the Beatles' manager

I think corporate intervention into the music business will probably be the most significant thing my generation left [behind]. The selling out of rock. I don't know what's gonna turn that around, or even if it can ever be turned around, or if people want it turned around. Maybe I'm just an old warhorse. Maybe it's time for rock 'n' roll to get out of the way for pop music, and let's just forget about rock 'n' roll and let the kids dance.

—JOHN MELLENCAMP, 1989

The whole business is built on ego, vanity, self-satisfaction, and it's total crap to pretend it's not.
—GEORGE MICHAEL

He gave us some good career tips. He said, "So you want to get into the music business? Good luck. They'll never let you work on your tan."

—NASH KATO, of Urge Overkill, recalling
advice from show biz veteran
Neil Diamond, 1995

To commit to a life in rock and roll—to open oneself up to the vagaries and hazards as well as the potential riches and other highs of the music business and lifestyle; to allow oneself to become or seek to be a celebrity—is to be extraordinary. It's not a matter of traveling to the beat of a different drum. It's being that different drummer.　　　　　　　　—BEN FONG-TORRES, rock journalist

Music can be a very humiliating business, but it's worth it in the end.　　　　　　　　—BRETT ANDERSON, of Suede, 1995

The Press

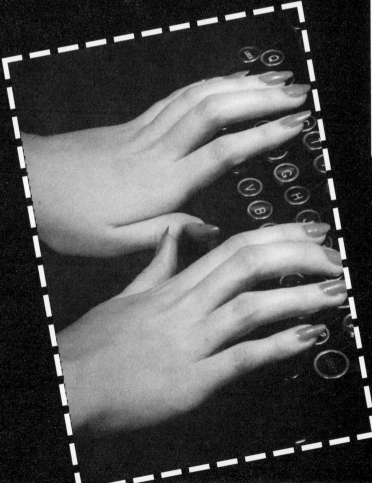

i read the news today, oh boy

What people write about you is not real. It's just their opinion. I've got some good reviews I can hang on my wall, and that's great. But what they write about me has nothing to do with me. —VAN MORRISON

I suppose if [Duran Duran] started getting good reviews we might stop selling records. —JOHN TAYLOR

I've got a review that calls me a genius right next to the one that calls me a jerk.
—BARRY MANILOW, 1988

If I ever see the word "indecipherable" again, I might vomit.
—MICHAEL STIPE, regarding a typical R.E.M. album review

They called me a bimbo in *Billboard* magazine and people would laugh at me in restaurants in L.A.
—TORI AMOS, recalling the reaction to her first albums, 1994

There was this one review that said things about me that boys said to me in the seventh grade . . . for instance—"slut." Yep, they called me that in this review. And "cheap coquette," a girl who made her way into lots of back seats in the drive-in theater, the kind of girl that made your father slip you a Trojan and pat you on the back and say, "Have a good time, don't stay out too late." I remember guys saying that sort of stuff to me when I was really young. I thought suddenly that the whole experience was repeating itself all over again. Those boys didn't understand me, and they didn't like me because I wasn't stupid and I was blunt and opinionated, but I was a flirt at the same time. They took my aggressiveness as a come-on. They didn't get it. And they didn't get *it,* if you know what I mean, so I guess they had to say things because they knew that was the only way they could hurt me. That review felt like junior high all over again.   —MADONNA

Sometimes I do get some constructive insights through [critics], to tell you the truth. Suspicions I have about my weaknesses can be confirmed.   —BILLY JOEL, 1982

Just because some critic doesn't think we're cool doesn't faze us. Well, it fazes us a little, or else we wouldn't say shit about it.
                                                     —ED KOWALCZYK, of Live, 1996

But I've never gotten over harsh criticism. I can never pick up a review and finish it if the guy doesn't like the album, 'cause the rest of my day is screwed up. It's so painful.
                                         —BARRY GIBB, of the Bee Gees, 1979

I will sit down with anybody that has criticized my work negatively; I will sit down with them and make them eat shit.
                                             —AUGUST DARNELL, of Kid Creole
                                             and the Coconuts

On any given night, we're still a damn good band. And on some nights, maybe even the best band in the world. So screw the press and their slagging about the Geritol Tour. You assholes. Wait until you get our age and see how you run. I got news for you, we're still a bunch of tough bastards. String us up and we still won't die.
                                         —KEITH RICHARDS, on the cracks about the
                                         Rolling Stones' latest tour, 1994

Touring is the perfect guise for the sport of serial killing. I do have a golden rule, though: I only pick the ones that will never be missed. It's curious how most of the victims were once music journalists. Their pathetic patter goes along the lines of "I used to be a rock critic once. I even reviewed a Banshees album without listening to it."

—SIOUXSIE SIOUX, of Siouxsie and the
Banshees, 1995

Visually they are a nightmare: tight, dandified Edwardian beatnik suits and great pudding-bowls of hair. Musically they are a near disaster, guitars and drums slamming out a merciless beat that does away with secondary rhythms, harmony and melody. Their lyrics (punctuated by nutty shouts of yeah, yeah, yeah!) are a catastrophe, a preposterous farrago of Valentine-card romantic sentiments.

—a Newsweek review of the Beatles' Ed Sullivan
Show appearance

It was my role to be a bit more the cheerful chap than the others. I was always known in the Beatles as the one who would sit the press down and say, "Hello, how are you? Do you want a drink?"

—PAUL McCARTNEY, 1974

Never let a photographer take you outside. That just means he has a tree he wants to take a picture of and he needs someone to stand in front of it. You don't see Madonna out in fuckin' cornfields!

—PAUL WESTERBERG, of the
Replacements, 1995

It must be hard for the critic and the journalist to define or describe a melody, to convey a musical idea in a literal way.

—BILLY JOEL, 1982

> **Rock journalism is people who can't write interviewing people who can't talk for people who can't read.**
> —FRANK ZAPPA (1940–1993)

Writing about music is like dancing about architecture.

—ELVIS COSTELLO

Oh, I love to lie. That's one of my favorite things in the world, coming up to somebody, especially press people, and telling them some enormous lie that couldn't possibly be true.

—ALICE COOPER, 1973

Even stars get tired of talking about themselves. Some of them can talk intelligently, but a lot of them can't even hold a decent conversation. They know nothing but rock, and not a lot about that. It makes it difficult to get a decent interview. A lot of times, you'll be lucky to get more than muttering and stuttering.

—BILL GRAHAM (1931–1990),
concert promoter

So many strange things are written about me that it really doesn't affect me anymore because it's so ludicrous. . . . In some ways it's good protection. I'd rather have people writing things that were completely off the mark because then I stay a lot more private.

—P. J. HARVEY, 1995

Every year my press agent sends me everything that's been written about me. It's quite amusing to look through. . . . A certain percentage of it is true but the perception is a complete fabrication. That's consoling—it's not me!   —STING, 1989

Nobody deserves to have their personal life pried into like I did, and no one deserves to hear me whine about it so much.

—KURT COBAIN (1967–1994), of Nirvana

I'm sick to death of reading about U2.
—EDGE, of U2, 1989

Sometimes when I see my face taking up a whole page of a magazine, I hate that guy. —EDDIE VEDDER, of Pearl Jam

Interviewers don't talk about my singing as much as they talk about my lifestyle. —JANIS JOPLIN (1943–1970)

People have a right to ask questions and dig deep when you're hurting people and things around you. But when I haven't talked to anybody in years, and every article I see [about me] is dope this, junkie that, whiskey this—that ain't my title. Like, "Hi, I'm Layne, nail biter," you know? My bad habits aren't my title. My strengths, my talent are my title. —LAYNE STALEY, of Alice in Chains, 1996

If I had been a straight-A student my whole life and had rapped about Jesus coming back to save us all, I wouldn't get no media. The motherfuckers wouldn't give a fuck about me. But since I'm telling the truth, and been through what I'm stressing and know what I'm talking about, I'm a threat. Because the motherfuckers have to respect the fact that this motherfucker knows what they know, but has a little more power than they do. That makes them feel I'm a threat, the same way Malcolm [X] and Martin [Luther King] were. —SNOOP DOGGY DOGG, 1995

Never underestimate the value of bad press; in the end it's about the same as good press because it makes people talk about you. It's only when they don't write about you at all that you're doing something wrong. —PAUL WESTERBERG,
of the Replacements, 1995

Fighting the American press is like disobeying your parents, because they're so pompous. Critiques in the States usually have the tone of book reviews a lot of the time. In live concert reviews they treat you like opera!—"Mister Costello did this" . . . and so forth. —ELVIS COSTELLO, 1983

Interviewers could be pretty mean. In England I was asked, "How does it feel to be the chubbiest Osmond?" —JIMMY OSMOND, 1995

Get plenty of article that is just pure foolishness. You have a guy come talk to you for a whole week, and him go an' write something for please the Devil. —BOB MARLEY (1945–1981), 1975

It's embarrassing to read the drivel that comes out of your mouth sometimes. —JAMES TAYLOR, 1979

I just naturally say things to shock, not necessarily to offend. It's like pulling the tablecloth off the table to disarm everybody.

—MADONNA

I've become more aware of the possible consequences of what I say to the press. —STING

Doing interviews can sometimes mess up my head. It makes me feel dirty. It's frustrating how the press recycles a quote to death. I guess I'll just have to throw out some new crazy statements, but it's hard to plan that sort of thing.

—JULIANA HATFIELD, who hasn't been able
to live down a statement she made during an
interview claiming to still be a virgin, 1995

You wanna know why I don't like the press? Did you see the last cover story that's been done on us? If I ever see the guy who wrote it again, I'm gonna beat him up. He made us look like wimps! He was around backstage on the last night of our spring tour, and he heard us bitchin' a little about how the road sucks. And he made it seem like we don't like to tour. That we're too big and rich to want to do it anymore. A lot of kids will read that and think it's true!

—STEVEN TYLER, of Aerosmith, 1979

I tend not to read things that are printed about me anymore. Because from one article to the next you wouldn't know they were talking about the same person.

—ANI DiFRANCO, 1995

Past Imperfect

mommy's all right, daddy's all right, they just seem a little weird

y family] didn't stop me from doing anything that I wanted to do. I had my first fuck in the drawing room of my mother's house. The whole incredible thing about my parents is that I just can't place their effect on me, and yet I know that it's there. When people find out that my parents are musicians, they ask how it affected me. Fucked if I know.   —PETE TOWNSHEND, 1968

I came from a family of losers . . . and I've rejected my family as something I don't want to be like.

—STING

Let's face it, you are your parents, whether any of us like it or not.
—JOHN MELLENCAMP, 1987

If [my parents] were dead, I think that would have been easier. The fact that they were an hour away was a living rejection.
—BILLY CORGAN, of the Smashing Pumpkins, 1994

My relationship with my family was something totally different ten years ago. Ten years ago I would have said, "Dysfunctional family. Worthless, middle-class, boring American family." We didn't hug, we didn't say we loved one another, we didn't have any of that. Now

I look back on my family almost like I'm ready to re-establish my relationship with them. —DAVE PIRNER, of Soul Asylum, 1995

I was always embarrassed because my dad wore a suit and my mother wore flat pumps and a cozy jumper while my friends' parents were punks or hippies. —SHIRLEY MANSON, of Garbage, 1997

For some time, my parents have been saying that I belong on the end of a rope. —DAVID LEE ROTH

When I was young what we read was the Bible and UFO magazines. . . . My dad was equal parts God and Hagar the Spaceman in Mega City. My mother taught me fantasy: my mother's like a real hip Scheherazade. Between the two of 'em, I developed a sensibility. —PATTI SMITH, 1976

Oh God, everything I have is gone! —ELVIS PRESLEY (1935–1977), at his mother's funeral, 1957

My mother used to tell me about vibrations. I didn't really understand too much of what that meant when I was just a boy. To think that invisible feelings, invisible vibrations existed scared me to death. —BRIAN WILSON, of the Beach Boys, 1976

Looking at my mother gives me confidence. She had nine children before she was 28. And she raised seven of us on her own. So it's really nice to able to say to her, "Here, Mom, would you like this dress?" —DOLORES O'RIORDAN, of the Cranberries

When my mother, who was single, had me, it was a scandal because she didn't want to be a housewife. She didn't want to wear makeup, she wanted to let her hair hang down and wear her eccentric clothes and she was just an outcast. —BJÖRK

Some parents want their kids to be doctors or lawyers. [My mother] . . . wanted us to be in the numbers racket. —RICK JAMES

I was trying to convince my mother to buy me this guitar and she said, "What songs are you going to play?" and I said we would write our own. She said, "You want to write songs and you can't even play an instrument!" —TOM PETTY

I feel a little self-conscious doing weird feedback solos and grabbing my weenie with my mom standing there [in the audience].

—CRIS KIRKWOOD,
of the Meat Puppets, 1997

I think of her nearly every single day. If I never do anything really wrong, it's all because of her. She wouldn't let me do anything wrong. —ELVIS PRESLEY (1935–1977), on his
mother, 1962

[My mother would] cry about my blindness and the hopelessness of my ever seeing, but I told her I wasn't sad. I believed God had something for me to do.

—STEVIE WONDER, 1995

She's me 'ousekeeper. And she's a great cook. You see, I was cradle snatching. I snatched her daughter at 16, right out of a convent school, and she 'adn't learned 'ow to cook yet, so I said, "Get your mother up 'ere." She's been living with us for about a year now.

—KEITH MOON (1946–1978), of the Who,
on his mother-in-law, 1971

You know what I remember? I remember him coming home from the hospital and taking me out to the backyard, just him and me, and teaching me the last three verses to "This Land Is Your Land" because he thinks that if I don't learn them, no one will remember. He can barely strum the guitar at this point. . . . His friends think he's a drunk, crazy, and they stick him in a puke green room in a mental hospital.

—ARLO GUTHRIE, on his legendary father,
Woody, who died from Huntington's
disease, 1977

I grew up under the piano. My father talked to me with his fingers, playing Debussy and Beethoven. He didn't talk to me much one-to-one as a human being, but I'm glad he didn't. That's where my emotion comes from.   —STEVEN TYLER, of Aerosmith, 1990

[My father] was a professor of music but also a professor of humanities. So he taught me phenomenology as well as classical music. Of course, I totally rebelled against classical music. I thought it was squaresville.   —THURSTON MOORE, of Sonic Youth

My father was a school teacher before the war. He taught physical education and religious instruction, strangely enough. He was a deeply committed Christian who was killed when I was three months old. A wrenching waste. I concede that awful loss has colored much of my writing and my world view.

—ROGER WATERS, of Pink Floyd, 1988

My daddy is my biggest fan. He's a minister, you know.

—ALICE COOPER

> **What I do now is all me dad's fault, because he bought me a guitar as a boy, for no apparent reason.**
> —ROD STEWART, 1988

My daddy knew a lot of guitar players and most of them didn't work, so he said, "You should make your mind up to either be a guitar player or an electrician, but I never saw a guitar player that was worth a damn!"   —ELVIS PRESLEY (1935–1977)

By the time I came along, [my father] wanted a boy. He wasn't too pleased with my sex from the beginning. So, perhaps during an Oedipal phase in my life, I went after him in a very matter-of-fact way, thinking I had to win this man's love. I may even have felt that it was going to be important for all my relationships with men.

—CARLY SIMON, 1981

My father didn't give me advice, he just gave me orders.

—MADONNA, 1991

All our lives, from the time we were born, my brothers and I raced to be what my father used to say we were: winners. "So go out there and be winners!" he'd yell. I mean, really scream. And he'd turn and tell me, "Write this song and make it a Number One record!" When your father tells you to do something, you do it, because all you've ever known since you were a little baby was that he was boss.

—BRIAN WILSON, of the Beach Boys

One of the first memories I have was my dad coming back from Vietnam in his uniform when I was three years old, and my mom telling me that he was my dad.

—JERRY CANTRELL, of Alice in Chains, 1996

I used to say to me auntie, "You throw my fuckin' poetry out, and you'll regret it when I'm famous," and she threw the bastard stuff out. I never forgave her for not treating me like a fuckin' genius or whatever I was when I was a child.

—JOHN LENNON (1940–1980), 1971

Just before his death, [my grandfather] called everybody into his bedroom, and although he wasn't a religious person he said, "You know, I'm having a real bad beating of a time with the Devil." He was saying that the Devil wouldn't let him say a prayer to save himself. He'd built up this "I am a rock" pose and where had it gotten him? It stopped me cold to see my Grandpa so scared. Six hours later he was gone.

—JOHN MELLENCAMP, on his grandfather, who died from lung cancer, 1987

He collects cigarette butts and glues them together and makes pictures of naked ladies, then sprays the whole thing silver. His stuff was taking trash and making it art. I guess I try to do that, too.

—BECK, on his grandfather, 1994

I feel my son is an important part of the chain linking us with the past. Just as my father and mother made me strong as a person, educating me about struggle [of blacks for equality], hopefully I can do that for my son. You can be passive and selfish if you don't have a child. It's different when you have one. I have a stronger urge to make things better somehow through my rapping.

—ICE CUBE, 1993

I always worried about my son, about him having the first-generation money. You want him to have the same street background you had. I think it's important for a male child to understand what the street's about, because the sensibility of the world is really driven by the street. . . . It's okay for your daughters not to experience that, but for a boy, I think you can set him back by not letting him have that part of his life.

—QUINCY JONES, record producer, 1995

My son, just because of his presence, keeps telling me there is a tomorrow, there is a future, and there's no point in screwing up today; because every day that you screw up is going to have an effect, karma-wise, on the future.

—DAVID BOWIE, 1983

You leave home to seek your fortune and, when you get it, you go home and share it with your family.

—ANITA BAKER

They say domesticity is the enemy of art, but I don't think it is. I had to make a decision: am I going to be just a family guy, or should I go up to London three nights a week, hit the nightclubs, occasionally drop my trousers, and swear a lot in public? I made my decision, and I feel okay with it. Ballads and babies—that's what happened to me.　　　　—PAUL McCARTNEY

What you can do with an electric guitar is nothing compared to what you can do with a penis. After you've created life, writing a single doesn't seem like much of an accomplishment anymore.

—ANDY PARTRIDGE, of XTC, on how his
daughter changed his musical perspective, 1989

Show business is very much an illusion. Chauffeur-driven limos, the sparkle, the popularity, it was all an illusionary job. What's real is what I have now, a husband and three kids; I'm a den mother, I'm perfectly content.

—KATHERINE S. SCHAFFNER,
of the Marvelettes

I make my son waffles. I take him to school. I'm really no different from the mom that lives in Idaho.

—ME'SHELL NDEGEOCELLO, 1997

I was freaked out about if I had a baby, would I start writing songs about being a mother, like Joni Mitchell?

—KIM GORDON, of Sonic Youth, 1994

It's a weird thing. My kids seem to be more mature and older than I am now somehow. They've gotten ahead of me somehow. But they're very patient with me.

—JERRY GARCIA (1942–1995), of the
Grateful Dead

Children is wonderful, a part of my richness.

—BOB MARLEY (1945–1981),
1975

I got lost on one of the Bible verses that said, "Be fruitful and multiply." I didn't read no further.

—SOLOMON BURKE, father of 21 children

[I would sacrifice] whatever necessary. I would drop my career like that if I had to. What is more important than guiding the upbringing of your offspring? If anyone's got anything more important, please step forward. I defy anyone.

—TED NUGENT

i was raised in Leavenworth, Kansas, by
parents who were good parents. But all they
wanted was for everything to be OK and not talk
about anything. As I went into my adolescence and
was also gay, I could take all this crazy energy, all
this "I'm going mad" energy, and play it, sing it,
yell, scream, and people would applaud.

—MELISSA ETHERIDGE, 1994

When I was growing up, there were two things that were unpopu-
lar in my house. One was me, and the other was my guitar.

—BRUCE SPRINGSTEEN

I really used to jam. I used to pull out all these different pots of different sizes and different tones and these spoons, and I used to
drive my mother absolutely nuts. Since then I've known what I
have to do.   —LENNY KRAVITZ, 1995

I used to sit in the basement with my guitar and freeze. Freeze. Just
fucking shiver because it was so cold in the basement and my
mother wouldn't heat it up beyond a certain point because we
couldn't afford it. . . . And I'd play my fucking guitar with my
numb fingers, and just fucking hate it. I hated my life, I hated my
existence, I hated everything.   —BILLY CORGAN, of the Smashing
Pumpkins, 1995

I realized right away I could write songs because I could have experiences without even having them! And I'd run to the guitar, and I'd

cry, and my parents would leave me alone because it was like, Don't come in the door. A great artist is at work here. I kept a guitar at the foot of my bed.

—STEVIE NICKS, 1989

It was a time of intense emotion in that the boys were going to one front or the other of the war, more than likely to be killed. And so when they were drinking, they'd drink with gusto, and when they were singing, they sang with all their hearts, and I got to sing with these guys.

—ROY ORBISON (1936–1988),
on growing up around musicians during
World War II, 1989

Y'see, the birth of rock 'n' roll coincided with my adolescence, my coming into awareness. It was a real turn-on, although at the time I could never allow myself to rationally fantasize about ever doing it myself. I guess all that time I was unconsciously accumulating and listening. So when it finally happened, my subconscious was ready.

—JIM MORRISON (1943–1971), 1969

I went straight from the Boy Scouts to rock 'n' roll. Fancy that!

—STEVE WINWOOD, 1989

I had no place to live, and I spent all my money on alcohol and drugs. . . . My mom wouldn't let me sleep in her basement any more. . . . I had burned all my fucking bridges. The people who loved me were like, "Dude, it's not fucking cute anymore." And that was it. Dude, it was hopeless. So I moved into a Salvation Army shelter for a few weeks to get myself together, and when I got out, that's when Rancid happened.

—TIM ARMSTRONG, of Rancid, 1995

Embarrassing. I was just so young. I feel like someone is peeling all my clothing off and I'm standing in Times Square and everyone is pointing at me.

—NATALIE MERCHANT, her reaction to
hearing her earliest songs

I used to take accordion lessons. I whipped out some heavy polkas and Beatles tunes 'n' shit.

—TOMMY LEE, of Mötley Crüe

Well, I picked up the guitar—or the ukulele—at the age of 18 with no ambition to have a career in music, just to accompany bawdy drinking songs.   —JONI MITCHELL, 1995

It's [been] seven years of playing in clubs, dragging your equipment upstairs, dealing with my dad, all those doubts, people writing stuff about us, the band almost falling apart—you look at all those things, and you can't help but go, "We fucking did it."
    —BILLY CORGAN, of the Smashing
    Pumpkins, 1995

I played bump-and-grind joints, where the stripper genuinely had a goddamned horse in her act.   —BOB SEGER, on his first gigs, 1983

The old guys were really getting into it. And it's fun to play for people like that. It's more of a compliment to have someone that doesn't listen to rock music say, "Hey, you guys are really good. I don't know what it is, but I liked it."
    —FRANK BLACK, of the Pixies, on playing at
    strip clubs during the early days, 1989

My fondest memory is of having people walk by me to get to the bathroom and knocking the microphone stand—every night I'd have a bloody lip. These were, like, old-man corner bars, not rock 'n' roll places. . . . All the local kids would come in, and most of the old men would get mad and leave. But some would stay. They'd like it, you know: "I'm not goin' home! Hell with the wife! I *like* this!"
    —BRIAN SETZER, of Stray Cats, on their early
    gigs, 1983

Some of those club owners were crazy. There was one guy, pulled out a gun one night and shot an amplifier. Can you see it? Smoke curling up to the ceiling. Absolutely quiet. And he says, "I told you to turn it down."   —BRUCE SPRINGSTEEN, on his early
    performing days

I was writing songs even in my teens. The trouble was, you couldn't play them at shows—some clubs even had rules about it. So we'd say, "Here's a song by Santana" and play one of our own, and no one would know.   —TOM PETTY, 1990

We were such a band in those early years—just driving around in a truck, pulling into town and wreaking havoc. Being shitty adolescent punk rockers. . . . It was as close to a Kerouacian adventure as any of us had ever had. We would drive somewhere and someone would pay us $200 to make noise for an hour and a half. What could be greater? —MICHAEL STIPE, of R.E.M.

I wanted to be a nun. I saw nuns as superstars. . . . When I was growing up I went to a Catholic school, and the nuns, to me, were these superhuman, beautiful, fantastic people.

—MADONNA, 1991

A doctor. And I wanted to be a time traveler and build a time machine, but I wasn't scientifically endowed, so I became a cult figure instead. —ROBYN HITCHCOCK, on what he wanted to be when he grew up, 1995

I had good memories of who I was before I was five, and then I became everybody else's idea of who I was. Before I was five I was at the piano most of the time, and kind of oblivious to stuff. . . . I distinctly remember having no inhibitions creatively at that age.

—TORI AMOS

My first ever expression of emotion as a kid was fear. I was afraid of everything and everybody. I was afraid of this world, the next world, the heavens, the hells. —OZZY OSBOURNE, 1995

I came out jumping and I've been running ever since.

—JERRY LEE LEWIS

When I was a boy, I was the hero in comic books and movies. I grew up believing in that dream. Now I've lived it out. That's all a man can ask for. —ELVIS PRESLEY (1935–1977)

I've known I was going to a bigshot since I was four.

—PATTI SMITH, 1976

I just wanted to get the hell out of Ohio. I always knew that, since I was a junior in high school and this train used to go by. I know it sounds romantic, but it made me cry when I saw it. I just knew I had to be on that train someday.

—CHRISSIE HYNDE, of the Pretenders, 1980

I wouldn't have turned out the way I was if I didn't have all those good old-fashioned values to rebel against.

—MADONNA

Me and a million other dudes said "Later" to pickin' cotton. Moved North. Learned how to live in the city. Detroit, my Lord, what a place. Singin' in the streets, doggin' them clubs.

—WILSON PICKETT

I had two things to choose from. One was to stay there with the horses and cows and pigs and work on the farm and go to school and *not* be a musician. I felt from a kid up that wasn't my bag. I was gonna be a musician. I was different from any of the rest of the kids. I was *completely* different.   —JOHN LEE HOOKER, 1989

We were Poor. I'm spelling it with a capital P. . . . We were on the bottom of the ladder looking up at everybody else. Nothing below us 'cept the ground.   —RAY CHARLES

I come from the heart of the Chicago ghetto. I've been through the same shit that Ice-T and them have been through. It's been a long time, but you don't forget that journey. Ever. Bel-Air is where I live, but my soul's not up here.   —QUINCY JONES, record producer, 1995

"Working class punk" is what we are. We all had blue collar upbringings. We all came from very humble backgrounds and saw our families struggle to support us. I saw my mom hold down weekend jobs after working all week. She worked as an Avon lady and a keypunch operator just so we [could] have shoes.

—LARS FREDERICKSEN, of Rancid, 1995

A year ago I was living in a shed behind a house with a bunch of rats, next to an alley downtown. I had zero money and zero possibilities. I was working in a video store doing things like alphabetizing the pornography section for minimum wage.

—BECK, 1994

I've never filled out a job application, never stood in line for an interview or struggled to write a resume. I never worked in a video store rewinding tapes or in a 7-Eleven pouring Slurpees. I admire Eddie Vedder's work ethic, but I'm sorry I didn't pump gas.

—DAVE NAVARRO, of Red Hot Chili
Peppers, 1995

We had nowhere to go. So what did we do? We threw bricks at passing cars. That's an old favorite. That's something you can do in the flats. I did all the usual things like nicking cars and that. But everybody does. It's just something to do.

—JOHNNY ROTTEN, of the Sex Pistols, on
his impoverished youth, 1978

I came out of that whole doo-wop, street-corner environment, and I'm not ashamed to tell anybody. I didn't know a kid in my life who didn't steal an apple from a peddler.

—FRANKIE VALLI, of the Four Seasons, 1977

> **I was a wiseguy, I talked too much, I spoke out of turn. And I was a notorious unachiever.**
>
> —JERRY GARCIA (1942–1995), of the Grateful Dead,
> on his high school days, 1989

Oh, I would refuse to sing the school song; I would refuse to salute the flag; I would wear weird things to school; I would get in trouble all the time, and get thrown out of school. I did things that were pretty notorious. I used to be in the marching band in high school; I played the snare drum. They threw me out because they caught me smoking under the bleachers with my maroon uniform on.

—FRANK ZAPPA (1940–1993), on his high
school days, 1979

A couple of teachers would notice me, encourage me to be something or other, to draw or paint—express myself. But most of the time they were trying to beat me into a fuckin' dentist or a teacher.

—JOHN LENNON (1940–1980), 1971

My life has been what you might call an uneventful one, and it seems there is not much of interest to tell. . . . I have many hobbies. Some of these are hunting, fishing, leatherwork, reading, painting and playing Western music. I have thought about making a career out of Western music if I am good enough but I will just have to wait to see how that turns out. . . . Well, that's my life to the present date, and even though it may seem awful and full of calamities, I'd sure be in a bad shape without it.

—BUDDY HOLLY (1936–1959), from a
homework assignment he wrote during his high
school years; Holly died in a plane crash at the
age of 23

Baseball, though, was the big thing with me. I can remember, clear as a bell, sitting on my father's lap in our living room and listening to a 1947 Yankee game on the radio: boy, I loved the Yankees. My father once took me to a Dodger game at Ebbets Field—in 1949— and I was so ashamed of being there that I wore a Lone Ranger mask so nobody would recognize me.

—PAUL SIMON, 1975

I used to love to look at the moon at night. I would go out in the backyard and stare at it. It just fascinated the hell out of me. And another thing that fascinated me that would scare most people is lightnin'. When I was a kid, I thought that was pretty. Anything like brightness, any kind of lights.

—RAY CHARLES, recalling his childhood
before he became blind, 1973

The Meaning of Life

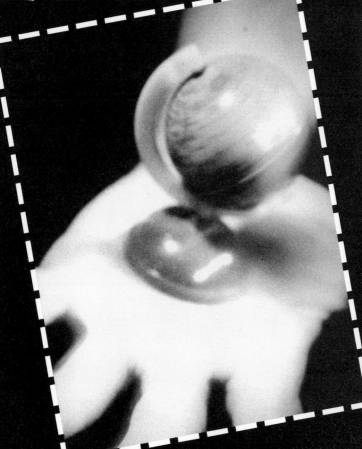

philosophy is a walk
on a slippery rock

e're not the descendants of philoso-
phers. We're the children of court jesters.

—JIMMY BUFFET, 1995

You are born into this world effectively like somebody getting into a taxi—you don't know quite where the taxi is going.

—ROBYN HITCHCOCK, 1995

I do not believe or comprehend the world I live in.

—BRUCE SPRINGSTEEN

I'm interested in anything about revolt, disorder, chaos—especially activity that appears to have no meaning.

—JIM MORRISON (1943–1971)

We're constitutionally incapable of taking much seriously.

—BOB WEIR, on the Grateful Dead's approach to living, 1989

Nowadays we're more into staying in our rooms and reading Nietzsche.

—ROBERT PLANT, on the philosophical pursuits of Led Zeppelin, 1975

It's abysmal thinking of how many years there are to go, millions of them. I just play it by the week.

—JOHN LENNON (1940–1980)

I'm still searching for an angel with a broken wing. It's not easy to find them these days. Especially when you're staying at the Plaza Hotel.

—JIMMY PAGE, of Led Zeppelin, 1975

I believe that someday we're gonna find our way, that there's angels and they hear us praying. I believe in all these things. But if someone were to ask me, "Do you believe it for yourself, Chris?" I'd say, "Well, not for me." It's not gonna happen for me, but I believe in it and want it so bad for somebody. The fact that it happens for somebody is enough. —CHRIS ISAAK, 1995

We should be more concerned with what's bloody right! You'll be spiritually better, and that's what counts when you're lying on your deathbed. —SINÉAD O'CONNOR, 1990

What's wrong with the system is that it's not based on the spirit. People put their faith in money. But you can't pay $9 to get your heart massaged. And you can't get a face lift for your heart. Your heart cannot drive a Ferrari. You know what I mean?
—G. LOVE, of G. Love and Special Sauce, 1995

The world is craving spirituality so much right now. If they could sell it at McDonald's, it would be there. But it's not something you can get like that. You can only wake up to it, and music is the best alarm. —CARLOS SANTANA, 1995

I call myself a hopeful cynic.
—TRACY CHAPMAN

I don't think I'm getting more cynical, I've just got more evidence to back up my cynicism. —FRANK ZAPPA (1940–1993), 1982

I'm afraid of intellectuals—they bring dissention and envy and jealousy. —ELVIS PRESLEY (1935–1977)

I've really learned that I don't know much.
—EDDIE VAN HALEN

They say, "You contradict yourself a lot." But life is a paradox. I don't know all the answers. I just call 'em as I see 'em.

—ICE-T

We were born to struggle, to face the challenges of our lifetime, and, ultimately, to evolve to a higher consciousness.

—QUINCY JONES, record producer

I don't always have a clear idea of what I want. I have to struggle to find out because it might be important. . . . As I'm struggling to figure that out, the struggle takes the form of music and it's beautiful.

—JULIANA HATFIELD, 1995

I never knew that life was so serious and hard and cruel. You can't depend on anything at all.   —RICKI LEE JONES, 1979

I've come to realize that life is not a musical comedy, it's a Greek tragedy. I'm an adult now; I've paid my admission fee to this ordeal, and I'm disappointed I didn't get a brass band in the deal. You know better than to believe there'll ever be a brass band backing up your struggles and celebrating your victories, but you never stop hoping, and that's part of what keeps life so sad, so bittersweet.

—BILLY JOEL, 1982

Well, living is difficult, period. Being happy and serene and all that stuff doesn't get necessarily any easier just 'cause you're more mature—or sober.   —BONNIE RAITT

I don't think happiness is necessarily the reason we're here. I think we're here to learn and evolve, and the pursuit of knowledge is what alleviates the pain of being human. And everybody is in pain, but if you're learning something, your mind is diverted elsewhere.

—STING, 1983

To live is to suffer; to survive is to find some meaning in the suffering.   —ROBERTA FLACK

I think it's more important to deal with life as it comes along than sit around pondering one's personal philosophy. You'd be dead before you ever had a chance to implement it! What useful things you find out in this world, you invariably find out on foot, on the move. You can't wait. —ELVIS COSTELLO, 1983

It's marvelous and confounding, this life, but I'm learning to adapt.
—STEVE WINWOOD, 1989

One thing I reckon, though, is that life can be really great—if you're not enjoying it, you may as well check out now.
—MICK JONES, of the Clash, 1995

There is no perfection . . . this is a broken world and we live with broken hearts and broken lives but still that is no alibi for anything. On the contrary, you have to stand up and say hallelujah under those circumstances. —LEONARD COHEN, 1995

Life is about sex and risk, but that doesn't mean that's all life is . . . they're merely a starting point. I think it can expand its horizons a little more than that—but I think a life of sex and risk can be very satisfying as well. I've had a lot of it myself. But I would add relationship to that. —DAVID BOWIE, 1983

I'm one of those fools who believes anything is possible. It's probably a real innocence or stupidity on my part. . . . But with U2, I suppose we're dreamers and, so far, our dreams have come true. This can give you a false perspective that the impossible is always possible. —BONO

What's been great about the human race gives you a sense of how great you might get, how far you can reach.
—JERRY GARCIA (1942–1995), of the Grateful Dead

I read once in some spiritual context that the bad part of you is your human limitations, and the good part of you is God.
—GEORGE HARRISON, 1987

You see cowards a lot when you're doing something that's honest, because you remind them of their own dishonesty.
—SINÉAD O'CONNOR

I believe that you learn more from failing than from succeeding. Yet we have a built-in fear of failure, a shame of failure, which I think is pretty harmful. —PETER GABRIEL, 1986

Maybe there are people who really believe that whole "I'm okay, you're okay" stuff. I say, "If I'm okay and you're okay, then who got us into this mess?" *Show* me the guy, and I'll pound him to smithereens. —T-BONE BURNETT, 1983

The most important thing in the world to me now is being a kind person. I don't think there's anything more hard-core than being loving. —FLEA, of Red Hot Chili Peppers, 1995

Be strong, believe in freedom and in God, love yourself, understand your sexuality, have a sense of humor, masturbate, don't judge people by their religion, color, or sexual habits, love life and your family.

—MADONNA

Always let them see you sweat.

—PAUL WESTERBERG,
of the Replacements, 1995

But try to break as many [rules] as possible if you can. Not just for the sake of doing it but for the feeling of freedom that you get when you just step a little bit out and kind of go "Whoa!"

—LAURIE ANDERSON, 1995

What's important about doing good in life is detail. God looks after the big stuff—or Nature does, if you're not religious. Nature can look after Niagara Falls, the Antarctic, and Space. What we can look after are tiny details. —PETE TOWNSHEND, 1989

Two things you don't do, you don't beg and you don't steal.

—RAY CHARLES, 1973

Don't moan about being a chick, refer to feminism or complain about sexual discrimination. Write a loosely disguised song about it instead and clean up. Do not insist on working with females. Get the best man for the job, and if they happen to be female, great.

Shave your legs, for Christ's sake. Don't take advice from people like me. Do your own thing. —CHRISSIE HYNDE, of the Pretenders, from her list of do's and don't's for chick rockers, 1994

The way I view it, the only way to find out what's going on in life is to go through it full force with your head down and to smack into a few walls on the way. That's the only way to learn. Then, hopefully, after a while, you figure out which one not to keep hitting.

—JERRY CANTRELL, of Alice in Chains, 1996

If anyone gives you criticism that starts off "you should" or "you shouldn't," walk away immediately.

—PAUL WESTERBERG,
of the Replacements, 1995

Love what you do. On any level, love it, do it because you have to do it. Do it for whomever you can, wherever you can, and what happens beyond that is just icing on the cake.

—MELISSA ETHERIDGE, 1995

Mold your world, don't let it mold you.

—DARYL HALL, of Hall & Oates, 1987

In art and dream may you proceed with abandon. In life may you proceed with balance and stealth.

—PATTI SMITH, from the intro to her
collection of poetry, *Early Work*

Say what you want, but if you get your ass kicked, don't get mad. Suffer the penalties.

—CHUCK D

Keep your nose clean and your chin up, even if it requires surgery.

—RAY DAVIES, of the Kinks, 1995

Keep God first. Visualize a goal and try to reach it, and if you can't reach it, find something other than the negative. Because the negative is a long stretch behind the wall—trust me.

—SNOOP DOGGY DOGG, 1996

Knowing that everything's futile but still fighting, still raging against the dying of the light—that's what motivates me all the time. . . . If you hold that sense of futility in your head for too long, it can begin to eat into you. You can still be aware of it but find a place for it where you can actually exist comfortably and enjoy things. So it still doesn't matter if we all die, but given that, you may as well do something that's really good fun.

—ROBERT SMITH, of the Cure, 1989

I think a jump rope can be as helpful to a depressed person as methadone maintenance or psychotherapy.

—JAMES TAYLOR, 1979

The young and crazy often need aspankin' and aplankin'.

—LITTLE RICHARD

They should read the Bible, they should read *Lolita*. They should stop reading Bukowski, and they should stop listening to people who tell them to read Bukowski.

—NICK CAVE, his suggested reading list for high school students

You can never underestimate the stupidity of the average person.

—GLENN DANZIG, 1994

People are really somethin'. They're walking books, all of them. Sometimes you'll only meet them once, but you'll never forget them. So you try to enjoy them. That's why, even if you're in the ladies' room, you should always talk to the woman next to you.

—CYNDI LAUPER, 1984

You learn nothing from a lie. Even as you discover a deliberate untruth, it always only confirms what you already knew but refused to face. —ROGER WATERS, of Pink Floyd, 1988

Don't take yourself too seriously, that's incredibly important. Don't start believing what everyone else is saying about you—good or bad. Keep a grip on reality. —BRETT ANDERSON, of Suede, 1995

So all I do is love, I don't fall in love. Love as honest as you can, as strong as you can, but never, ever fall in love. You'll remember I told you that as long as your memory lasts.

—BARRY WHITE, 1994

Cultivate hatred. It is your greatest asset.

—MALCOLM McLAREN, on the best way to achieve success in the rock industry

"Shit or get off the pot, Seger! No crybabies allowed in rock 'n' roll!" I never got better advice.

—BOB SEGER, recalling words of wisdom from Ted Nugent during Seger's early performing days, 1983

Jimi said, "The best thing you can do, brother, is turn it up as loud as it'll go."

—BILLY GIBBONS, of ZZ Top, recalling advice given to him by Jimi Hendrix, 1984

Just write. Don't worry where the tune comes from. I just pick up tunes I heard before and change them around and make them mine. Put in a couple of fast notes for one slow one, sing a harmony note 'stead of a melody, or a low note for a high one, or juggle the rests and pauses—and you got a melody of your own. I do it all the time.

—WOODY GUTHRIE (1912–1967), his songwriting advice to Bob Dylan

If you're gonna write songs, you've gotta have a life. It's as simple as that.

—DON HENLEY, 1990

you gotta serve
somebody

still believe in God.

—MADONNA, 1991

I've always thought there's a superior power, that this is not the real world and that there's a world to come. That no soul has died, every soul is alive—either in holiness or in flames.

—BOB DYLAN

I'm not into religion, but I have a good grasp on my spirituality. I just believe that I'm not the greatest power on this earth. I didn't create myself, because I would have done a hell of a better job.

—LAYNE STALEY, of Alice in Chains, 1996

I know there's a true and breathing God. A lot of people don't believe in that, but I know there's no way it can't be. . . . It's so true that there is a God, when you break it down: the universe, the beauty of the world, the sun.

—MICHAEL JACKSON, 1989

I think man has ruined God.

—BONO, 1987

I believe God gives every man a choice. Every man has a choice to do what he will, bad or good, right or wrong, black or white, rich or poor. —LITTLE RICHARD

It's like Christ said, "You'll all do greater work than I will." He wasn't trying to say, "I'm the groove, man, and you should follow

174

me." He was out there . . . trying to hip everybody to the fact that they have Christ within. —GEORGE HARRISON, 1987

I am the strings, and the Supreme is the musician.
—CARLOS SANTANA

I don't feel very well equipped for the job I've been given as a singer or songwriter. Maybe that's why I have the faith I do, because I'm very dependent on the idea that God has given me a gift. Therefore it's His responsibility to get me through it!
—BONO, 1987

I think [the Beach Boys] were always spiritually minded and we wrote music to give strength to people. I always feel holy when it comes to recording. —BRIAN WILSON

I sit down and listen to "What's Going On" and I have no idea where it all came from. How did I ever do it? I know it was channeled from God, but I have this nagging feeling that if I had to do it over again, I couldn't. —MARVIN GAYE (1939–1984)

You know, I'm not a believer in any organized religion. I don't call myself a Muslim or a Christian or a Buddhist. But I do believe in one God. And he's been watching over me. I mean, by now I should be in jail, living on the streets or dead.
—COOLIO, 1995

But with a few exceptions, I'm skeptical of churches. I worry that they can't deal with issues like AIDS. I worry that the most racist places in the world can be places of worship. We have to build our churches in our hearts. —STEVIE WONDER, 1995

I don't have to visit God in a specific area. I like Him to be everywhere. —MADONNA, on why she doesn't go to church

I don't go to church at all, but I'm somehow sure I'll become more interested in it later in my life, as that seems to be the general way things go as you age. —BRYAN FERRY, of Roxy Music, 1985

As a Methodist, I remember going to church four times a week, and I did that until I was 21. . . . I used to get really pissed off that my life was so dictated by when this Jesus guy was born and when he was dying every year. I felt really resentful that I couldn't get on with my own life, because I was so busy with his.

—TORI AMOS, 1994

I was raised in the church. I went to Sunday school. I went to the morning service, and I went to night service, and I went to revival meetings. So hearin' this good singin' in the church and also hearin' the blues, this was the only way I could sing.

—RAY CHARLES

We were a religious family, going around together to sing at camp meetings and revivals. Since I was two years old all I knew was gospel music; that was music to me. We borrowed the style of our psalm singing from the early Negroes. We used to go to these religious singings all the time. The preachers cut up all over the place, jumping on the piano, moving every which way. The audience liked them. I guess I learned from them. I loved the music. It became such a part of my life it was as natural as dancing, a way to escape from the problems and my way of release.

—ELVIS PRESLEY (1935–1977)

I gave up rock 'n' roll for the rock of ages! I used to be a glaring homosexual until God changed me!

—LITTLE RICHARD, 1957

I think we are due for a revival of God awareness. Not a wishy-washy kind of fey, flower-child thing, but a very medieval, firm-handed masculine God awareness where we will go out and make the world right again.   —DAVID BOWIE, 1976

> There is nothing written in the Bible, Old or New Testament, that says, "If you believe in Me, you ain't going to have no troubles."
>
> —RAY CHARLES

As an atheist you have to rationalize things. You decide first of all that you will not ask Daddy—meaning God in all of his imagined forms—for a helping hand when you're in a jam. Then you have to try and make some sort of sense out of your problems. And if you try and find you can't, you have no choice but to be good and scared—but that's okay!   —BILLY JOEL, 1982

Here's the thing: You can believe in God or not, but a lot of what's being said there is pretty true. Look at the golden rule. That's the first thing I was taught: Do unto others as you'd have them do unto you. If we could all just do that, what a great place the world would be. One crummy little rule, and none of us can follow it.

—JOHN MELLENCAMP, 1985

I don't believe in a benign intelligence. I don't think there is a father hovering over us, like a child over a model village. Or maybe there is, but it's literally a child. I don't think it's anything smarter and brighter than us controlling our destinies.

—ROBYN HITCHCOCK, 1995

Once you're a Catholic, you're always a Catholic—in terms of your feelings of guilt and remorse and whether you've sinned or not. Sometimes I'm wracked with guilt when I needn't be. . . . We're all gluttons for punishment.   —MADONNA

I went to Catholic school through the eight grade. I hated it. They didn't let me wear Levis. These nuns were ignorant. Nuns are the worst fascists.   —LINDA RONSTADT, 1983

In the third grade a nun stuffed me in a garbage can under her desk because she said that's where I belonged. I also had the distinction of being the only altar boy knocked down by a priest during Mass.

—BRUCE SPRINGSTEEN

I used to go to Mass with my friends, and I viewed the whole business as a lot of very enthralling hocus-pocus. There's a guy hanging up on the wall in the church, nailed to a cross and dripping blood, and everybody's blaming themselves for that man's torment, but I said to myself, "Forget it. I had no hand in that evil. I have no

Original Sin. There's no blood of any sacred martyr on my hands. I pass on all of this."   —BILLY JOEL, 1982

That's one of the problems I've had with Christianity. It's humorless, and you're born in debt. You owe Jesus one because he died for you long before you were ever conceived.

—ROBYN HITCHCOCK

Christianity will go. It will vanish and shrink. I needn't argue about that. I'm right and will be proved right. Jesus was all right, but his disciples were thick and ordinary. It's them twisting it that ruins it for me. We're more popular than Jesus Christ right now.

—JOHN LENNON (1940–1980), 1966

Christ was a punk rocker.

—BILLY IDOL

The devil is a very generous mon—he'll give you everything for your soul! Hear me, he's a very generous mon, a very tricky mon.

—BOB MARLEY (1945–1981), 1975

But you can't take God and the devil along together. Them two fellows, they don't communicate together so well. They don't get along so well. The devil believes in one way, and God believes in a different way. Now, you got to separate them two guys. How you gonna do it? You got to follow one or the other. You can't hold God in one hand, the devil in the other one. You got to turn one of them loose. Which side do you think is best?

—SON HOUSE

If I'm going to hell, I'm going there playing the piano.

—JERRY LEE LEWIS

Band
Life

here are times we'll be sitting together when we'll look at each other and laugh and go, "Right, we're the new pop heroes." It's just stupid. The whole position of being in a rock band is stupid. It's really one of the most embarrassing ways to make a living that you could possibly imagine.

—PETER BUCK, of R.E.M., 1989

I thought being in a band was an antiestablishment lifestyle. It's only ever been my interest to maintain that, and to maintain my freedom as a bum. I don't want to be recognized; I don't want to be hassled. I just want to play guitar in a rock 'n' roll band.

—CHRISSIE HYNDE, of the Pretenders

A rock 'n' roll band needs to be able to get under people's skin. You should be able to clear the room at the drop of a hat.

—PAUL WESTERBERG, of the Replacements

When you start a rock 'n' roll band, you've gotta fake it till you make it. You begin by doing what you love, and what you love is usually what some other people have already done. It just depends on how much of a fool you make of yourself along the way to finding your own sound—assuming you find it.

—STEVE TYLER, of Aerosmith

We had nothing against the big groups. It was just the lack of opportunity for anybody who wasn't a big rock star. I always felt that a lot of those groups just sort of left you as they found you:

You'd go to the concert and wouldn't feel any more inspired than before—they just took you and they fleeced you. . . . There wasn't any thinking involved—it wasn't challenging in any way.

—MICK JONES, of the Clash

We're not media manipulators or fashion kings or this week's bunch of bad boys. What we want to do is play the music.

—NICK HEXUM, of 311, 1997

Well, it seems there are a lot more nerds in bands than there ever were. The nerd quotient is really high. Which is kind of comforting in a way.

—TOM GORMAN, of Belly, 1995

The best bands are tribes.
—HENRY ROLLINS, 1995

It's not easy being in a group. It's like marriage without sex. The only lubricant we have is our music.

—STING, on playing with the Police, 1983

But it's hard to be married to one person; it's harder to be married to five. Everybody goes in different directions.

—RIC OCASEK, of the Cars, on the difficulty of being in a band, 1991

We'd been going full force, just running at top speed with our eyes closed. We had been way too close for too long, and we were suffocating. We were like four plants trying to grow in the same pot.

—JERRY CANTRELL, of Alice in Chains, on the band's near breakup, 1996

I think the Who's relationships are more about need than desire. We don't necessarily want to be dependent on one another, but we are.

—PETE TOWNSHEND, 1982

I didn't care if it was the Beatles, I was getting out.

—GEORGE HARRISON, 1987

It really was difficult to know what to do, 'cause you were either going to say, "Okay, I've been a Beatle, and now I'll go back to the sweet shoppe or do something else with my life." Or, "I'll try to continue in music!" But then the thought came, "Yeah, but you're gonna have to try and top the Beatles," and that's not an easy act to follow.

—PAUL McCARTNEY, 1987

[The band] has been our home for our whole adult lives. It served us all well—us, the audience and, hopefully, humanity. We did it with everything we had. It was a magnificent creation. We thought we should go out with dignity.

—MICKEY HART, of the Grateful Dead, on
disbanding after Jerry Garcia's death, 1996

I was a bitch a lot of the time. I was like the snotty little sister. I spent most of the last tour in the back lounge of the bus with the door shut.

—NATALIE MERCHANT, recalling her last
years with 10,000 Maniacs, 1995

The Who will never just fizzle out. They'll go out with a huge explosion.

—PETE TOWNSHEND, 1976

It must seem strange that we do the same thing with the same boys all these years later. It seems strange to me. But it's like when you get drunk at a bar and wonder later how you got home. You know where you are—you're home—but how did you get there? That's the mystery.

—CHARLIE WATTS, of the Rolling Stones, on
the Stones's longevity, 1994

If we get into the Top 10 or whatever, then great, but it's not our only ambition. Besides, I think kids in America resent it when a band comes over from Britain, proclaiming it is the next big deal. Our whole approach has been, "Just take us for what we are. . . ." We don't go over [to the U.S.] flag-waving, saying, "You should like us because we came from the land of Lennon and McCartney."

—NOEL GALLAGHER, of Oasis, 1995

We reckoned we could make it because there were four of us. None of us could've made it alone, because Paul wasn't quite strong enough, I didn't have enough girl appeal, George was too quiet, and Ringo was the drummer. But we thought that everyone would be able to dig at least one of us, and that's how it turned out.

—JOHN LENNON (1940–1980)

The great thing about U2, and probably about Adam [Clayton] and myself more than anyone else, is that we struggle with our musicianship all the time. We don't know what to do. We don't know what the format is, we don't know what a great rhythm section is supposed to do; we're still discovering. . . . It's the struggle, the fight to get it right, that makes U2 what it is. The day U2 stops fighting is the day that U2 will not be the band it is now.

—LARRY McMULLEN, 1987

We were so awkward, musically speaking, when we got together as a band. We couldn't really play our instruments or anything. But that didn't stop us from playing them.

—BONO, 1987

I thought, what the hell, all the people in my other bands couldn't "play" either! I kind of look for that on purpose, it makes everything unique when people don't have previous training.

—KAT BJELLAND, of Babes in Toyland, 1994

The government doesn't want you to have a good time, and sometimes your parents don't want you to have a good time. Guess what, baby? The Black Crowes want you to have a motherfucking good time.

—CHRIS ROBINSON, of the Black Crowes

Our band doesn't have any rock 'n' roll lifestyles, I'm afraid. We're horribly mundane, aggressively mundane individuals. We're the ninjas of the mundane, you might say.

—ANDY PARTRIDGE, of XTC

We were upper middle class brats that had anything we wanted. The whole end is that we are what we are—a living social criticism.

—ALICE COOPER, describing himself and his
band members

In almost any situation people tend to focus on whoever's in front of the microphone, whereas in a lot of cases, that person isn't really the anchor of the band or the leader of the group. It's like . . . it's like a democracy, and I'm the president.

—LES CLAYPOOL, lead singer of Primus, 1995

The Pistols are presenting one alternative to apathy and if you don't like it that's just too bad. It's not political anarchy . . . it's musical anarchy.

—JOHNNY ROTTEN,
of the Sex Pistols, 1978

> **We never had an us-against-them attitude.**
> **Why does being in a rock band or being a musician make**
> **you such an exclusive person?**
> —THURSTON MOORE, of Sonic Youth, 1994

We're only a band. We're not bringing a scene or a counterculture with us. All we ever wanted to do was play rock 'n' roll, music that people can relate to. We come from a background of punk rock, but we're not walking down the street with a shopping cart with "Punk Rock" on it, you know?

—BILLIE JOE ARMSTRONG,
of Green Day, 1995

People are starting to realize that CSNY was never a band. We were four individuals you could juggle in any combination, but would always be just that—individuals. People have always wanted us to be in a band, to have something to believe in—and that's bullshit. They wanted to believe that we were actually spokesmen for today's society. That's fucked. But it's more naive than fucked.

—GRAHAM NASH, of Crosby, Stills, Nash
and Young

We didn't really have a band with Cream. We rarely played as an ensemble; we were three virtuosos, all of us soloing all the time.

—ERIC CLAPTON

It's a living thing, this Fleetwood Mac, a source stronger than its various members.

—CHRISTINE McVIE

[Duran Duran is] as good an example as anybody of what the early '80s were. Excessive, bright, and full of hope. And not realizing that you were gonna get the bill at the end of the decade.

—NICK RHODES, of Duran Duran, 1995

Soul Coughing is about a groove. There's nothing to understand. It goes straight to the butt. That's the destination, the butt.

—M. DOUGHERTY, of Soul Coughing, 1997

We want to be phalluses ramming in the butthole of pop.

—GIBBY HAINES, of Butthole Surfers

We want to be the band to dance to when the bomb drops.

—SIMON LE BON, of Duran Duran

I like to think of [The Velvet Underground] as Clearasil on the face of the nation.

—LOU REED

Primus is like a greased pig. It's not an easy thing for a lot of people to grab on to.

—LES CLAYPOOL, of Primus, 1995

We just did our own thing, which was a combination of rock 'n' roll, and Fellini, and game-show host, and corn, and mysticism.

—FRED SCHNEIDER, of the B-52's

We're the McDonald's of rock. We're always there to satisfy, and a billion served.

—PAUL STANELY, of Kiss

We say it's Lesbian Seven. We say it's a level of consciousness when you get to level seven in meditation. We say it's lubrication, a love jelly called L7. There's actually a guitar amp called L7. . . . There's also a panty size L7—large seven—very apropos for this band.

—SUZI GARDNER, of L7, on the inventive
explanations she's given about her band's name
(the actual origin of the name is a '50s slang
term for "square"—as in not hip)

I always figured that, you know, everyone had a bush. It wasn't specifically female. Anyway, we all come from bush.

—GAVIN ROSSDALE, of Bush, on how he
came up with the name for his band, 1995

You'd have to be numb or dead not to get excited about 20,000 people screaming.
                    —EDDIE VAN HALEN, 1995

And talk about power—that's a fucking trip. Put your hand up and 20,000 people scream.   —MICHAEL STIPE, of R.E.M.

It's a great feeling to be standing onstage and feel the power we have. We're the best band in rock 'n' roll. And we're going to stay there. Nothing else matters—the films, all the publicity. Just the music, that's the point of it all. That rush is too great to give up for anything.   —ROGER DALTRY, 1976

Onstage, I make love to 25,000 people, then I go home alone.
                    —JANIS JOPLIN (1943–1970)

Performers feed off the audience; sometimes you can tell how a gig's going to go at the moment you walk out onstage. You know what sort of electricity and energy is being put up toward the stage. I respond to that a lot. Sometimes you can generate that from nothing, but it is a lot harder.   —PETER GABRIEL, 1992

When you're on tour—and it doesn't happen all the time—sometimes you and your audience connect, just connect. . . . You feel this presence together with the audience and the band, which is just such a mind-blower. . . . You felt some sort of connection, where there was a whole wave of five or 10,000 people coming at you; you felt that you and the audiences were actually one. . . . That's what made me realize why all musicians keep playing.

—RINGO STARR, 1992

I love [touring]. It's me life. If I was to be deprived of touring. . . . I love being responsible for the enjoyment of a packed 'ouse. Knowing the four of us can go onstage and give enjoyment to that many thousand people, that's fucking something, man, that does me right in. If I'm good and the group is good, you can get 14,000 . . . 140,000 . . . get them on their fucking feet. Yeah. That's where it's at. That's what it's all about for me.

—KEITH MOON (1946–1978),
of the Who, 1971

[Performing] is like falling in love 20 times. I guess maybe having a baby would be something akin.

—JANIS JOPLIN (1943–1970)

I can't express myself in any conversation. . . . But when I'm up on stage, it's all the world. It's my whole life.

—JIMI HENDRIX (1942–1970)

The place I feel most comfortable these days is onstage; I can cut loose, and I'm so damned glad to be there.

—RICKI LEE JONES, 1979

When I get onstage, I don't know what happens. Honest to God. It feels so good, it's like the safest place in the world for me. I'm not as comfortable now as I would be onstage, because I was raised onstage.

—MICHAEL JACKSON, 1989

I guess that old piano is my best friend and the stage is my home. So if I don't stay on top I got nowhere to go.

—JERRY LEE LEWIS

I really got to say that I'm enjoying performing now more than I ever have in my whole career. For a long time, I didn't like my live performances, because I didn't feel they lived up to the significance of the records.

—STEVIE WONDER, 1995

I walk out to an empty stage; I'm very confident. This is what I do. I've done it so many times. I'm not at all nervous about going on. It feels comfortable and like home. But having said that, there's certain feelings that you get, you know: "Jesus, all those people!" There's a few empty seats sometimes, I see, and you say, "Oh, God, how many empty seats?"   —MICK JAGGER, 1994

Many a night I would be out onstage, and the intimacy of the songs against the raucousness of this huge beast that is an audience felt very weird. I was not David to that Goliath.
                                        —JONI MITCHELL, 1988

If you need your family and friends to come down and see you perform you're no performer.   —PAUL WESTERBERG,
                                        of the Replacements, 1995

I don't feel like I have the kind of personality that walks into a room and commands attention. Quite the opposite. . . . So I really think this whole performing thing is a way for me to basically just be myself—and have a microphone. To be myself and be louder than anybody else in the room. The songs are a vehicle for getting attention. I just hope, in the long run, they're good enough to be worth all the trouble.   —LYLE LOVETT, 1992

I . . . hated being on stage. I didn't care about singing to an audience but I didn't like people looking at my body.
                                        —DOLORES O'RIORDAN, of the
                                        Cranberries, 1994

I can't remember when [my agoraphobia] began exactly, but it would certainly happen every time I would try to go onstage, which is what made me think I had stage fright, when in fact it wasn't. It can get to me walking in the woods and in other nonstressful situations. It can attack me anywhere, and I'll be in a helpless state of anxiety. It was easy to focus my agoraphobia on one thing—the stage.   —CARLY SIMON, 1981

Every night [in 1978] I cried before I went on stage, but I still kicked ass when I got there.   —TED NUGENT

I would get so nervous before going on stage that I'd either get bombed or else my fingers would just freeze for most of the show. These days I just enjoy it and stay loose.

—JOHNNY MARR, of the Smiths, 1995

We were shitty in the beginning and we didn't care. We had the right idea. It was super punk rock. I wasn't nervous when I started playing. I'd already been stripping! If I could take my clothes off, I could definitely play this guitar in front of people. It was just fun. It's more nerve wracking now actually because people expect us to be really good!

—KAT BJELLAND, of Babes in Toyland, 1994

I could feel it starting to slip away. And I never wanted to be in front of people and have them pay to see me when I'm not 100 percent there. And if you feel that energy slipping away, then you've got to fold your deck—get out.

—NEIL YOUNG, 1988

I want out of the rock 'n' roll thing. I really do. It's a little late now. . . . Yet there I am, up onstage, performing my stuff. Certainly part of the reason originally was because no one else would. And I still think that to some extent. I do me really well.

—LOU REED, 1989

I felt people were listening more closely to my lyrics when I was playing clubs and in the folk scene than the larger audiences I've acquired do now.

—TRACY CHAPMAN, 1992

I believe that the life of a rock 'n' roll band will last as long as you look down into the audience and can see yourself and your audience looks up at you and can see themselves—and as long as those reflections are human, realistic ones.

—BRUCE SPRINGSTEEN

People have the need to set people above themselves. The stage is the illustration of that—the demigods. . . . I stand on a stage and I'm thinking, "What are you looking at me for, a damn old junkie hacking away at the guitar, what is this?" This must be a primal need.

—KEITH RICHARDS, 1992

There should be no difference between who's on stage and who's in the audience. We've tried very hard to break down those barriers. . . . We went on stage and we were totally honest. We weren't saying "Look at me. I'm great. I'm a superstar." We weren't saying particularly anything. We were going there and playing our music and anything could have happened when we were on stage.

—JOHNNY ROTTEN,
of the Sex Pistols, 1981

But I feel it's my duty to be as ugly and filthy as I am so the audience can experience what I've experienced. It's cathartic.

—MARILYN MANSON, 1997

Our audience is like people who like licorice. Not everybody likes licorice, but the people who like licorice really like licorice.

—JERRY GARCIA (1942–1995), of the
Grateful Dead, 1981

I depend on faces when I play. I have the light man backlight us so I can see people. Otherwise you get too inside your stuff, and how many times can you keep it interesting just for yourself?

—STEPHEN STILLS

. . . It's an unwritten rule for me that I don't want to see the audience.

—LINDA RONSTADT, 1995

I sing with my hair, I sing with my elbows. They can't see your eyebrows in the 93rd row. If you want to express happiness, you have to use your elbows for your eyebrows.

—DAVID LEE ROTH

Just point me to the piano and give me my money. In 15 minutes I'll have 'em shaking, shouting, shivering, and shacking.

—JERRY LEE LEWIS

I've always done me little theatricality bit of throwing me arms about with the music. Some people think it's a bit too much. Like when I was on *Ed Sullivan,* they surrounded me with thousands of dancers to keep me hidden.   —JOE COCKER

We knew we couldn't bite the head off chickens or unzipper our pants, wiggle our fannies around.

—ALAN OSMOND, on the Osmonds'
wholesome stage image, 1995

I always thought that if someone was gonna be interested in me as a performer, it was because of my songs—not so much the way I sing 'em.   —LYLE LOVETT, 1992

In my performances I don't consciously perform. I find when I consciously do it, I make mistakes. When I don't think and I just go for it, it all works out and it's basically flawless. When I second-guess it and think, "Well, what am I going to do here, or what note am I going to sing or which place am I going to move?" ultimately I always mess up.   —TEDDY PENDERGRASS, 1992

I certainly don't want to go on stage and just stand there and be ever so pretentious. I can't hardly sing, you know what I mean? I'm no Tom Jones, and I couldn't give a fuck. The whole thing is a performance of a very basic nature—it's exciting, and that's what it should be.   —MICK JAGGER, 1968

So just because I step onstage, does that mean I have to be your monkey? Does that mean I have to jump like you want me to jump and play the songs you want to hear?

—BILLY CORGAN, of the Smashing
Pumpkins, 1994

> **Just because you like my stuff doesn't mean
> I owe you anything.**
> —BOB DYLAN

I love to go on the stage and torture the audiences to the point where I know that they are all going to scratch and jump on each other. . . . I love to watch that and laugh at it. And they know it. The audiences are masochistic.

—ALICE COOPER, 1973

Historically, musicians have felt real hurt if the audience expressed displeasure with their performance. They apologized and tried to make the people love them. We didn't do that. We told the audience to get fucked. —FRANK ZAPPA (1940–1993)

The only reason we wore sunglasses onstage was because we couldn't stand the sight of the audience.

—JOHN CALE, of the Velvet Underground

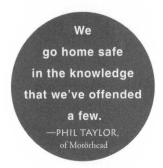

We go home safe in the knowledge that we've offended a few.
—PHIL TAYLOR, of Motörhead

I wish I [could] tell our audience that we don't hate them without sounding cheesy. —KURT COBAIN (1967–1994), of Nirvana

I tell people at every show that I love them, and I do. I give them everything I've got. —JERRY LEE LEWIS

Audiences never lie. They will tell you if they think you're any good or not. —BOB SEGER, 1995

Onstage, I've been hit by a grapefruit, beer cans, eggs, spit, money, cigarette butts, mandies, Quaaludes, joints, panties, and a fist.

—IGGY POP

It was a new attitude, better than the Marines, better than boot camp. I wanted the band onstage to be like soldiers, with me being the general, calling out the battle plan.

—JAMES BROWN, 1986

I like to play really stupid, dumb things, okay? Fuckin' obvious shit—but with a feeling of "We didn't know it was obvious. We were believing this."   —NEIL YOUNG, 1993

I lead a sexually alternative lifestyle (no, I won't elaborate) which sometimes seeps into my performance.

—DAVE NAVARRO, of Red Hot Chili
Peppers, 1995

We're running out of places to play, quite frankly. We're heading toward an "over-success" kind of extension.

—JERRY GARCIA (1942–1995), of the
Grateful Dead, 1991

I can do "Maggie May" now. And it's one of the highest points in the show.   —MELISSA ETHERIDGE, on being an openly
gay rock star, 1994

One time, somewhere in the South, I stood up in front of an audience and said, "There's something I want to say, but I don't know what it is."   —JOAN BAEZ, 1983

I'd like to see any son of a bitch follow that!

—JERRY LEE LEWIS; while opening for an act
he'd rather have been headlining, Lewis poured
lighter fluid over his piano and threw a lit
match on it

It 'appened when somebody got pissed off with the gig, with the way things were going. When Pete [Townshend] smashed his guitar, it was because 'e was pissed off. When I smashed me drums, it was because I was pissed off. We were frustrated. You're working as hard as you can to get that fucking song across, to get that audience by the balls, to make it an event. When you've done all that . . . and you've given the audience everything that you can give, and they don't give anything back, that's when the fucking instruments go, because, "You fucking bastards! We've worked our fucking balls off! And you've given us nothing back!"

—KEITH MOON (1946–1978), on why the
Who started smashing their equipment
onstage, 1971

I smash guitars because I like them.

—PETE TOWNSHEND

Sure. I've lost teeth. I mean I don't go out there to do myself a deliberate injury. But when you're on the road for that length of time, you're bound to twist an ankle or something. I once had splints on my fingers. I soon learned how to play slide with them, hah! I've jumped off amps and fallen ass over tit—made a complete fool of myself.

—ANGUS YOUNG, of AC/DC, on his energetic performances

Thank you [for the applause], we needed that. This is the second time we've ever played in front of people, man. We're scared shitless.

—STEPHEN STILLS, of Crosby, Stills and Nash, at Woodstock

You can leave if you want to. I'm just jammin'.

—JIMI HENDRIX (1942–1970), at Woodstock

I'm sorry, babe. I just ain't got no more.

—JANIS JOPLIN (1943–1970), to her audience after they refused to leave following a third encore

Well, [I felt] awful. I mean, just awful. You feel a responsibility. How could it all have been so silly and wrong? But I didn't think of these things that you guys thought of, you in the press: this great loss of innocence, this cathartic end of the era . . . That particular burden didn't weigh on my mind. It was more how awful it was to have had this experience and how awful it was for someone to get killed and how sad it was for his family and how dreadfully the Hell's Angels behaved.

—MICK JAGGER, on Altamont, where the Hell's Angels—acting as stage bouncers at a Rolling Stones concert—injured several audience members and killed one young man, 1994

We are modern-day cowboys—we ride into town, put on a show, take the money, hit the bar, take the ladies, and we're gone. And we do the same thing the next night in another place. The fans want to take a piece of you home, and their parents, they wanna throw us in jail, see us hung. So we're wanted: dead or alive.

—RICHIE SAMBORA, of Bon Jovi, 1987

Everybody does drugs . . . when you go on the road, there's nothing to do but do drugs and fuck. —STEVEN TYLER, of Aerosmith, 1984

> Being on tour sends me crazy. I drink too much and out comes the John McEnroe in me.
> —CHRISSIE HYNDE, of the Pretenders

We were doing a Motown revue—three days on the road, one day off. We were all on an old broken-down Trailways bus. We all had chaperones. We learned to eat sardines and popcorn for meals. A lot of times we were mistaken for freedom riders because we were a bunch of black people. Marvin [Gaye] and James [Brown] competed with different tuxedos. If Marvin wore a brown tuxedo, James would go and get a tuxedo with bigger ribbons down the side. Just like women. They were both so vain.

—MARTHA REEVES, of Martha and the
Vandellas, reminiscing about touring with
Motown acts during the '60s, 1995

With Soul Asylum, I learned to be on the road. And now, more than my friends, more than my band, I trust the road. If I lost everything, if my girlfriend dumped me and the band got rid of me, you know what I'd do? I'd just travel around like Woody Guthrie.

—DAVE PIRNER, of Soul Asylum, 1995

The road was our school. It gave us a sense of survival, it taught us all we know. There's not much left that we can really take from the road. . . . Or maybe it's just superstitious. . . . You can press your luck. The road has taken lots of great ones—Hank Williams, Buddy Holly, Otis Redding, Janis, Jimi Hendrix, Elvis. . . . It's a goddamn impossible way of life.

—ROBBIE ROBERTSON, of the Band

Between '86 and '90, I never unpacked my suitcase. That killed me. Everybody thought I was happening, but when I look at pictures from that time, I look beat up, with black circles under my eyes and everything.

—JON BON JOVI, on his hectic touring
schedule during Bon Jovi's hey-day, 1995

Just because you call an album *Highway to Hell* you get all kinds of grief. And all we'd done is describe what it's like to be on the road for four years, like we'd been. A lot of it was bus and car touring, with no real break. You crawl off the bus at four o'clock in the morning, and some journalist's doing a story and he says, "What would you call an AC/DC tour?" Well, it *was* a highway to hell. It really was. When you're sleeping with the singer's socks two inches from your nose, that's pretty close to hell.

—ANGUS YOUNG, of AC/DC, 1993

Thing is, next to the interviews and photographs, touring is my least favorite thing, but then I get drawn into it and the next thing I know, I'm out on the road.

—PAUL SIMON, 1975

[Simple Minds] toured too much in the '80s. The consequence of touring for us was that we could never write great songs on the road. When you're writing songs you need to really concentrate. The longer we were out on the road—and it got longer and longer—we would drift away from songwriting. . . . It was almost as though the songwriting was like being in school and going on tour was like being out for summer.

—JIM KERR, 1995

We were barred from so many hotels, the entire Holiday Inn chain, that we had to check in as Fleetwood Mac lots of times.

—RON WOOD, on touring with the Faces

I get bored, you see. There was a time in Saskatoon, in Canada. It was another 'Oliday Inn, and I was bored. Now, when I get bored, I rebel. I said, "Fuck it! Fuck the lot of ya!" And I took out me 'atchet and chopped the 'otel room to bits. The television, the chairs, the dresser, the cupboard doors, the bed—the lot of it. It happens all the time.

—KEITH MOON (1946–1978), of the Who,
when asked if he's really destroyed as many hotel
rooms while on tour as legend has it, 1971

There isn't a town in the world I haven't run amok in.

—JOE STRUMMER, of the Clash

[Our audiences are] acting out their version of how much freedom is there in America to go for a wild ride. What's left is, well, you can follow the Grateful Dead on the road. You can't be locked up for that, yet. So it's an adventure. And an adventure, as part of the American experience, is essential. It's part of what it means to find yourself in America. It's hard to join the circus anymore, and you can't hop a freight, so what do you do . . . Grateful Dead. These are your war stories, your adventure stories.

—JERRY GARCIA (1942–1995), 1989

and these poor girls, just sitting downstairs waiting to see whether they're gonna be picked up by somebody—they don't talk. . . . They just sit there in these little outfits that they've worked on for months, waiting for this thing to happen. And eventually, a Beatle will come by and pick one of them and, you know, drag her off to his lair.

—JOAN BAEZ, recalling a night she spent with the Beatles and their groupies, 1983

In one way, what genuinely turned me on was the music. There's a great relationship between the music and the body, and the musician who makes you feel so good, you quite often sleep with him out of gratitude. . . . I suppose in a way it's kind of "Thank you, what can I do for you?"

—JENNY FABIAN, from her autobiography, *Groupie*

They hung over rails with glassy eyes and pawed wildly at the air. Those near the stage held out their hands and screamed for Presley to kiss them. . . . It was frightening. Women have discovered burlesque—and they love it! He used the guitar the way Sally Rand used to use a bubble.

—review of an Elvis Presley concert, from the *Savannah Evening Press,* circa 1950s, describing Presley's effect on the women in the audience

I have seen people worked into frenzies. . . . I've seen 'em foaming at the mouth; I've seen 'em fall out. I've seen people screamin', cryin', can't stop. I've seen girls who just wanted to touch me, just screamin', lookin' at me, screamin' and fallin' out.

—LITTLE RICHARD, describing his audiences' reactions, 1990

Last night at the show this crazy blonde girl in the audience reached up and grabbed my hand, digging her nails right into the skin. Didn't she realize she was hurting me? I mean, shit, what did she want?

—FRANKIE VALLI, of the Four Seasons, 1977

This is very filthy, but when the hall empties out after one of my concerts, those girls leave behind them thousands of sticky seats.

—DAVID CASSIDY, 1972

You don't see an audience of young little girls screaming for us. So other people say, "Now that's a *real* band. That I like. It's real." 'Cause we aren't the prettiest things in the world. With AC/DC, it's not like we're here to steal your wife or your girlfriend and your daughter. We may *borrow* them.

—ANGUS YOUNG, of AC/DC, 1993

The way I've heard it described by the girls who have shared my bed and floor and bathroom is that, for them, it's not cheap sex.

—GENE SIMMONS, of Kiss, 1988

In the early days of [Black] Sabbath we used to have these marathon fuck-a-thons. I remember coming back from a gig on the first tour to my hotel room and hearing a knock on the door. I open the door, in walks a chick who fucks my brains out. Then she goes and a few minutes later there's another knock on the door and it's another chick. I ask her where they're coming from, and she says "the party." It happens one more time, three chicks in an hour, so I go and find the party on the roof-top and it was like Caligula: everything was going on up there. I just sat down with a gram of coke, a stiff drink, a joint, and a cute female messing around with my private parts. We all got the clap, crabs, all sorts of fucking things. I used to get so drunk that I'd wake up in bed with chicks I didn't remember being with . . . and I'd feel terrible because I was married! I always had a terrible conscience though, I'd always confess. I spent half my fucking life confessing!

—OZZY OSBOURNE, 1995

You know, I really do miss the old groupies. There used to be some great characters. Today, they're not as good looking as they used to be, and there's always the danger of catching the old full-blown.

—RON WOODS, of the Rolling Stones, 1994

I was looking for a new way to get pussy. I thought, "These Beatles guys get a lot of pussy; I'm gonna take this up."

—BILLY GIBBONS, of ZZ Top, 1986

> I wanted to perform, I wanted to write songs, and I wanted to get a lot of chicks.
> —JAMES TAYLOR

I am absolutely deluged with homosexual women at my concerts.

—JOAN BAEZ, 1983

I enjoy girls immensely, and I think they're part of what a rock concert should be. Whenever I go to a punk show and it's all boys on the dance floor, I think, "Hey, there's something missing here. Where's the sex?"

—TOM PETTY, 1983

You get the letters from 15-year-olds. They ask questions as if you're the second line of defense for their heads. They've become disillusioned with their parents and they think their teachers are assholes. . . . They're trying to contact you to see if you can enlighten them or be responsible for them and, of course, you can't. But when you read a letter, you think, can I reply? Do I shatter this person's illusions? Do I say, I'm just a normal guy?

—ADAM CLAYTON, of U2, 1987

They're expecting someone who's treading water to save them.

—EDDIE VEDDER, of Pearl Jam, on kids who
write him fan mail, 1993

There's some people that write [us letters] that have attempted to commit suicide and they've listened to our CD and they, you know, say they're feeling much better.

—BILLIE JOE ARMSTRONG,
of Green Day, 1996

It kind of scares me sometimes. It makes me wonder if, like, I'm really retarded in my emotional growth.

—JULIANA HATFIELD, on her mostly
teenaged following, 1995

Well, the thing that's wild about the Ramones is, we have the broad spectrum of an audience. I guess the average age now is 16 and younger, and then we have some of the original fans, older fans, kids into metal, thrash, hardcore, grunge. Then we have Republicans and Democrats and skinheads, and it's just this potpourri of people who wanna have a good time.

—JOEY RAMONE

Well, a girl can never get too many flowers. I'll listen to any reasonable offer. People seem to be pretty nice to me. All kinds of crazy people come to my shows. Sometimes, I feel like a musical missing link.

—SYD STRAW, on the admirers in her
audiences, 1995

We draw the ghetto, we draw the people ready to fight. We draw people who are ready to live. We draw the people who love righteousness.

—BOB MARLEY (1945–1981), 1975

What do they find so fascinating about these middle-aged bastards playing the same thing we've always played?

—JERRY GARCIA (1942–1995), questioning
the Grateful Dead's following, 1991

Somehow, by doing what I wanted to do, I manage to give people what they don't want to hear and they still come back. I haven't been able to figure that out yet.

—NEIL YOUNG

Our main audience is about 18 years old. People that age don't really understand music that much. . . . If they were really that musically hip, they wouldn't even like us.

—RICHARD BLACKMORE, of Deep Purple

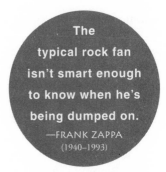

The typical rock fan isn't smart enough to know when he's being dumped on.

—FRANK ZAPPA
(1940–1993)

There are some that hang around outside [my] house and I tell them to piss off. They are quite funny, actually, because they love it when I get angry.

—SIMON LE BON, of Duran Duran, on Duranies, 1995

At first it was mostly teeny-boppers and a few local nuts hanging around. But a couple of years down the road, when people realized how weird we were, we really started drawing some creeps. We still do, I might add—Morrison wannabes show up on my doorstep all the time. And they always want to sing.

—ROBBY KRIEGER, of the Doors, 1994

Yeah, there's the element of, you know, football players and [people] that didn't like me back in high school. But it's hard for me to complain, especially when they're paying my rent. It *is* kind of strange to look out at some guy, like, wearing, you know, a Yale sweater going, "Fuck Yeah!"

—BILLIE JOE ARMSTRONG, of Green Day, on their latest typical audience members, 1996

Most of the new fans are people who don't know very much about underground music at all. They listen to Guns N' Roses; maybe they've heard of Anthrax. I can't expect them to understand the message we're trying to put across. But at least we've reeled them in—

we've got their attention on the music. Hopefully, eventually, maybe that music will dig into their minds. I don't really expect it to.

—KURT COBAIN (1967–1994),
of Nirvana, 1991

I think Kurt [Cobain] died more "punk rock" than when he started, because his music was embraced by so many people. He would play shows for jocks and realize how important his values were to him.

—NILS BERNSTEIN, publicist for the record
label Sub Pop

I know it's a love-hate thing. There are people that are big fans and people that really hate me. —AXL ROSE, of Guns N' Roses

When I started to do this "confessional reporting" [in my songwriting], partially it was artistic integrity, and partially I wanted to sabotage any worship that was setting up around me. If I was being worshipped, something was wrong. If you're worshipping things, it means you're not really leading a full life. It's healthy to admire; all of my musical growth has come out of admiration. But to worship, that's taking it too far. —JONI MITCHELL, 1988

i think the only reason I ever used drugs was to overcome shyness or self-doubt. . . . I think those substances were merely used as a little "instant courage," to overcome those feelings of "Who am I to be doing this . . . ?" I think some of the drug-taking was to blunt that feeling of undeservedness, because when you do coke, it makes you feel that everything you're saying is worthwhile and that everybody ought to listen. I didn't use drugs actually to create, but simply to buffer those feelings of inadequacy.

—DON HENLEY, 1992

I'm afraid of being mediocre, which, if you're a little bit loaded, you don't have to worry about. I think too much and judge too much and alcohol suspended that for a while, so it actually freed me up.

—BONNIE RAITT, 1992

To play sober, to play straight, is like going to the dentist, I suppose. You're very, very nervous until the actual thing is taking place, then you call on some reserve inside you which is just waiting.

—ERIC CLAPTON, 1992

I did it to myself. It wasn't society . . . it wasn't a pusher, it wasn't being blind or being black or being poor. It was all my doing.

—RAY CHARLES, on how he became addicted to heroin

I never thought I was wasted, but I probably was.

—KEITH RICHARDS

I was a successful junkie for about a year; the only reason I was able to stay healthy and didn't have to rob houses was because I had a lot of money.

—KURT COBAIN (1967–1994), of Nirvana

A thousand—I used to just eat it all the time.

—JOHN LENNON (1940–1980), on how many times he's tripped on LSD, 1971

Sometimes when I'm flying over the Alps I think, "That's all the cocaine I sniffed." We once tried to figure out how much money we spent on coke and alcohol. We were so disgusted that we stopped.

—ELTON JOHN, 1995

I think that what you find is that you've spent so much time and energy, which you didn't realize at the time, getting drunk or stoned.

—RINGO STARR, 1992

I've been healthy and I've been less than healthy, and healthy's much better. Less than healthy is more fun, but healthy is better.

—BONNIE RAITT, 1994

My credo: When I get scared and worried, I tell myself, "Janis, just have a good time." So I juice up real good, and that's just what I have.

—JANIS JOPLIN (1943–1970)

Never drank, never smoked. Fuck that. I can get happy by running.

—TANYA DONELLY, of Belly

I didn't take dope or nothing like that. The music turned me on.

—LITTLE RICHARD, 1990

I wanted to make a journey through the dark, on my own, to find out what it's like in there. And then come out the other end.

—ERIC CLAPTON, on why he used heroin, 1985

To get really high is to forget yourself. And to forget yourself is to see everything else. And to see everything else is to become an understanding molecule in evolution, a conscious tool of the universe.

—JERRY GARCIA (1942–1995), of the
Grateful Dead, 1972

I do smoke pot. . . . It's not great for things like memory, but within the relative security of the studio, in the womblike atmosphere where I know what's going on, it's very helpful. It breaks down the preconceptions you have about something; it allows you to hear it fresh.

—LINDSAY BUCKINGHAM, of Fleetwood
Mac, 1992

I smoke dope quite a bit and that really does help—not when I'm onstage or in the studio performing—it sort of fucks you up—but when I'm actually writing, because it opens your mind up. I mean you mustn't do it all the time because then it has the opposite effect.

—SINÉAD O'CONNOR, 1992

I used to take uppers and write, and I used to like that effect. In fact, I'd like to take uppers now and write because they give me, you know, a certain life and a certain outlook.

—BRIAN WILSON, of the Beach Boys

Alcohol in reasonable quantities has the same effect as lying in a bath; it deprives you of the jagged edges of your perceptions and senses.

—ROGER WATERS, of Pink Floyd, 1992

Mind-altering substances of one kind or another have been traditionally part of many cultures and have a place in shaping creativity. But I don't think it's something I would recommend to anyone nor that it is necessary. I think it's possible to get wherever you want to go without it. Perhaps sometimes it does short-circuit longer routes that maybe allow you to look through a window, perhaps at a state that might be arrived at through spiritual work. I'm not sure you actually get there. It's a very dangerous road.

—PETER GABRIEL, 1992

Part of the trap [of drugs and alcohol] is that they open the doors to unreleased channels or rooms you hadn't explored before or [been] allowed to open. —ERIC CLAPTON, 1992

[Drug use] doesn't have to exist for people to be able to broaden their level of consciousness. —STEVIE WONDER, 1995

Drugs can take you up, but they can also take you out. —SLY STONE, 1984

You find out so many interesting things when you're not on drugs. —BOY GEORGE, 1995

It's just that once you've had a taste of drugs, you like 'em and you want 'em. —BRIAN WILSON, of the Beach Boys

I don't think God necessarily put us here to be sober all the time, but I also don't think he put us here to be junkies. —COURTNEY LOVE, of Hole, 1995

I did cocaine basically for sex. My sexual fantasies were all played out while I was on cocaine. —ELTON JOHN, 1995

I don't drink because I'm an alcoholic. I drink because I love to party. —BRET MICHAELS, of Poison

It's weird, 'cause it'll sneak up on me. I'll see a bottle and like, have to stop myself. Soon as I get past that urge, it's okay. But I go to meetings and just really pay attention and get on my knees a lot, man. It's true. —STEVIE RAY VAUGHN (1954–1990), on being sober

I have a disease. It's called drug addiction, and I want to say I'm sorry to my friends, my band, my wife and family and the social ideals to which I have become a hypocrite. I ache to get well, to feel and to make more music.

—SCOTT WEILAND, of Stone Temple Pilots, from a statement read by friend Courtney Love on L.A. radio station KROQ, following Weiland's arrest for drug possession, 1995

I now don't subscribe to anything that I think you can get out of a joint, a bottle or a vial of pills. I don't think there is anything there that you can really make of use to humankind. There are certain things that will be triggered in your brain, for example, if you take a line of coke or smoke mescaline. Certain things do happen to your brain that are pleasurable for yourself alone. But to try to communicate that to other people is usually a waste of time.

—ERIC CLAPTON, 1992

I wrote about drugs, and I didn't think I was being unsafe or careless by writing about them. Here's how my thinking pattern went: when I tried drugs, they were fucking great, and they worked for me for years, and now they're turning against me—and now I'm walking through hell, and this sucks. I didn't want my fans to think that heroin was cool. But then, I've had fans come up to me and give me the thumbs up, telling me they're high. That's exactly what I didn't want to happen.

—LAYNE STALEY, of Alice in Chains, 1996

> I wanted to be the female version of Muddy Waters and Fred McDowell. There was a romance about drinking and doing blues.
>
> —BONNIE RAITT

There's nothing romantic, nothing grand, nothing heroic, nothing brave, nothing like that about drinking. It's a real coward's death.

—WARREN ZEVON

Boy, you could be the greatest guitar player that ever lived, but you won't live to see 40 if you don't leave that white powder alone.

—B. B. KING, to Stevie Ray Vaughn regarding Vaughn's cocaine habit

I woke up on a tour bus. I couldn't hardly get up. I was scared of everything—my friends. Just being awake, I was scared. . . . I was a total wreck. And I realized right then the only way to win this thing was to give up. Thank God that happened. I had a breakdown—only then was I able to ask for help instead of telling myself, "I'll make it through this." . . . People think that people on stage are bigger than life, stronger than life. That's what makes them so special to go see. But people on stage are not superhuman—that's a myth.

—STEVIE RAY VAUGHN (1954–1990), on
what it took to get him to sober up

I've always needed a drug to survive. The others, too, but I always had more, more pills, more of everything because I'm more crazy probably.

—JOHN LENNON (1940–1980), 1971

To some I'm a junkie madman who should be dead, and to others, I'm a mythical genius.

—KEITH RICHARDS

An herbsman is a righteous mon who enjoy the sweetness of the earth and the fullness thereof. Him just smoke herb like the Bible say, and commit no crime.

—BOB MARLEY (1945–1981), on the religious
qualities of smoking marijuana, 1975

I think [drugs and alcohol] almost have to be done with a spiritual, ritualistic [feel], like a prayer.

—JONI MITCHELL, 1992

Somebody has to let [kids] know that it's not hip anymore to do drugs, that there will always be pressures and times in your life when you'll need answers, but that coke and the rest offer nothing—no outlet, no information. And, believe me, you're only as good as your information.

—BOB SEGER, 1983

If drugs are making your decisions for you, they're no fucking good. . . . If you're far enough into whatever your drug of choice is, then you are a slave to the drug and the drug isn't doing any good.

—JERRY GARCIA (1942–1995), of the
Grateful Dead

Alcohol is something I've stopped doing. That and cocaine are not creative things.

—LINDSAY BUCKINGHAM, of Fleetwood
Mac, 1992

I don't wake and bake like I used to.

—DEAN WEAN, of Wean, refuting the
rumor that he smokes excessive amounts
of marijuana, 1995

In the morning is my favorite time [to smoke pot] . . . although my girlfriend gets mad at me, because if I'm on tour, and I get stoned, I forget to call.   —EDDIE SPAGHETTI, of Supersuckers, 1995

The most deadly thing about cocaine is that it separates you from your soul.   —QUINCY JONES, record producer

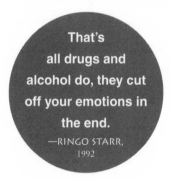

That's all drugs and alcohol do, they cut off your emotions in the end.
—RINGO STARR, 1992

My first drug experience was sniffing glue. We tried it, and moved on to Carbona. That's why we wrote songs about it. It was a good high, but it gave you a bad high. I guess it destroys your brain cells, though.   —JOHNNY RAMONE, of the Ramones

When I was a practicing alcoholic, I was unbelievable. One side effect was immense suspicion: I'd come off tour like Inspector Clouseau on acid. "Where's this cornflake come from? It wasn't here before."   —OZZY OSBOURNE

You think I'm an asshole now, you should have seen me when I was drunk.   —JOHN MELLENCAMP

How can you enjoy your life when you get up in the morning and you're surrounded by empty bottles and the mirror's covered in smears of cocaine and the first thing you do is lick the mirror?
—ELTON JOHN, 1995

I definitely have a responsibility to talk negatively about heroin. It's a really evil drug. I think opiates are directly linked to Satan.
—KURT COBAIN (1967–1994), of Nirvana

The last thing I could bear is to feel guilty about smack.

—KEITH RICHARDS, responding to his
heroin possession charges

What's the difference between selling dope because there's a demand, or an oil man who pollutes the world?

—ICE-T, 1991

I'm not saying that I'm a saint, but I've never had a drug problem. Yet I saw the cocaine thing become this insidiously destructive juggernaut in the lives of friends. When I thought the whole coke mess couldn't get worse in the late '70s, that's when it exploded as a hemispheric plague, wrecking governments in South America and threatening to ruin a generation here. Next, I pick up *Newsweek* and read about grammar school kids buying crack with their allowance!

—BOB SEGER, 1983

Drugs and sex go hand in hand when you're a rock 'n' roll musician. Whereas if I were a violinist, it might be a little different.

—SLASH, of Guns N' Roses

I seem to remember the wine was the best and the drugs were good and the women were beautiful, and man, we seemed to have an endless amount of energy. Endless stores of energy. Hangovers were conquered with Bloody Marys and aspirin, you know what I mean? There were no two-day purges or hiding in your bed. It seemed that you bounced back, you were resilient.

—GLENN FREY, of the Eagles, recalling the
drug-riddled music scene of the '70s, 1990

If you can remember anything about the '60s, you weren't really there.
—PAUL KANTER, of Jefferson Airplane

If you stuck my stays in rehabs together you're looking at two years solid. . . . The '70s was full of coke and the '80s was full of programs. When I first went to the Betty Ford Center I was very surprised they didn't have a bar there. . . . I thought they taught you how to drink like a gentleman.

—OZZY OSBOURNE, 1995

In the late '60s everyone got into experimenting and questioning the rules. All of a sudden it became a clean slate. The effect of that was in the '70s, when everyone would just do a bunch of coke and freak out and swap wives and go to Plato's Retreat. The aftermath of that is the '80s, which gives you music you can go to Alcoholics Anonymous by. —MIKE D., of the Beastie Boys, 1989

It's hard to believe that [we] did so many drugs for so long. . . . You know, it was eating and drinking and taking drugs and having sex. It was just part of life. It wasn't really anything special. It was just a bit of a bore, really. Everyone took drugs the whole time, and you were out of it the whole time. It wasn't a special event. —MICK JAGGER, 1994

Obviously, there was drugs in rock 'n' roll, and the sex ain't too bad. But I don't know anybody that actually lives like that all the time. I used to know a few guys that did that, but they're not alive anymore, you know? And you get the message after you've been to a few funerals. —KEITH RICHARDS

Amid the lunacy of it all, we did have some pretty good times; but in the end, when you're just sitting in your room for two weeks at a time having cocaine put under your door, and not eating, and drinking bottles of whiskey, there is no fun in it.
—ELTON JOHN, 1995

I was the instigator—I was responsible for him [being] back on the road after 1978. And after three tours of America, he was a bloody junkie. I felt responsible for that. It was really hard to live with, and I just don't want to do it anymore. I mean, I think the world of that guy. I think enough of him to stop the Who.
—ROGER DALTRY, explaining how Pete
Townshend's drug abuse was the reason Daltry
broke up the Who, 1982

I think we just sort of grew out of drugs. The drugs aren't necessary now. They were then, as a crutch. We went through just about everything . . . the bloody drug corridor. . . . Eventually we stopped fucking about with the chemicals and started on the grape. Drinking suited the group a lot better. When we started drinking, that's when it all started getting together.

—KEITH MOON (1946–1978), of the Who; Moon died from an overdose of antialcoholism tablets; 1971

The only way we made it was with a great big old bag of Mexican reds and two gallons of Robitussin HC. Five reds and a slug of HC and you can sleep through anything.

—BUTCH TRUCKS, of the Allman Brothers

The sheer number of people who wind up becoming junkies after signing a major label deal. I sometimes wonder whether some major labels prefer their artists to be strung out on dope so that they can control them. —JELLO BIAFRA, of Dead Kennedys, 1996

In my line of work, if you drank all the drinks, and took all the drugs you were offered, you would die. Simple as that.

—ELVIS COSTELLO

Of course, though, becoming a heroin addict is the worst thing for a woman to do. —MARIANNE FAITHFUL, 1994

I read [an] article once where they said that heroin slows down aging. People in the Orient have been smoking opium for centuries, and they live to be 100 or more. If they could separate the pure essence from the drug's addictive properties, they say it could suspend you at the age where you were when you began taking it!

—FRANKIE VALLI, of the Four Seasons, 1977

I started using stuff when I was 16 and first started in show business. Every experience I've had—good and bad—has taught me something. I was born a poor boy in the South, I'm black, I'm blind, I once fooled around with drugs, but all of it was like going to school—and I've tried to be a good student. I don't regret a damn thing. —RAY CHARLES, on his past heroin habit

Friends & Enemies

with a little help from my friends

Ialways wanted the fire of Springsteen. I always wanted the melodies that Van Morrison could write. I always wanted the heart of Joni Mitchell. And I wanted the guitar rhythms of Keith Richards.
—MELISSA ETHERIDGE

I'd like to get something together, like with Handel, and Bach, and Muddy Waters, flamenco type of thing. . . . If I could get that sound, I'd be happy.
—JIMI HENDRIX (1942–1970)

So Jimi started to play. He stood on a chair in front of me—just Jimi, on a chair, playing at me . . . like "don't fuck with me, you little shit."
—PETE TOWNSHEND, on Jimi Hendrix

He spent a lot of time combing his hair in the mirror.
—ERIC CLAPTON, on his first time meeting Jimi Hendrix

He thought he was some kind of voodoo child. He wasn't no voodoo child; he was a nigger who played good guitar and wrote some good songs.
—RICK JAMES, on Jimi Hendrix

Finally in New York, the yelling for us got so bad during Jimi's set that he walked off the stage. He was in the middle of a number. He threw his guitar down, flipped everyone the bird, said, "Fuck you," and walked off the stage. I was standing with Mickey Dolenz, and I turned to Mickey and I said, "Good for him."
—MICHAEL NESMITH, of the Monkees, recalling how Jimi Hendrix was heckled while opening for a Monkees concert

I didn't want the Who to follow [Jimi Hendrix at the Monterey Festival]. . . . I was saying to Jimi, "For fuck's sake, Jimi, listen to me. I don't want to go on after you. It's bad enough that you're here. It's bad enough that you're gonna fuck up my life. I'm not gonna have you steal my act. That's the only thing I've got. You're a great genius. The audience will appreciate that. But what do I do? I wear a Union Jack jacket and smash my guitar. Give me a break. Let the Who go on first." —PETE TOWNSHEND, 1994

Uh, yes, Jimi Hendrix. He was my guitar player, and you know, we didn't know he could play with his mouth. One night I heard this screamin' and hollerin', and they were screamin' and hollerin' for him! I thought they were screamin' for me. But he was back there playin' the guitar with his mouth.

—LITTLE RICHARD, when asked if he'd ever been upstaged by anyone, 1990

> The most exciting moment of my life was appearing on the stage with Little Richard.
> —KEITH RICHARDS

There is something elegantly sinister about the Rolling Stones. They sit before you at a press conference like five unfolding switchblades; their faces set in rehearsed snarls; their hair studiously unkempt and matted; their clothes part of some private conceit; and the way they walk and they talk and the songs they sing all become part of some long mean reach for the jugular.

—PETER HAMILL, journalist

Quite simply, I feel that the Stones are the world's best rock 'n' roll band. —PETE TOWNSHEND

I don't think the lyrics are that important. I remember when I was very young, I read an article by Fats Domino which has really influenced me. He said, "You should never sing the lyrics out very clearly." —MICK JAGGER, 1969

[Mick Jagger is] not unlike Elton John, who represents the token queen—like Liberace used to.   —DAVID BOWIE, 1976

I admire Mick Jagger for being a very good exponent of PR. He really knows his PR. I think the PR has overshadowed the music in recent years, but you've got to give him credit. . . . It's Disneyland. You're not going to see the Rolling Stones really—you're going to see Disneyland.   —RAY DAVIES, of the Kinks, 1995

He's the last of the line. He's the end of that whole folk tradition.
—DAVID MARSH, rock journalist,
on Arlo Guthrie

[The Band] sung epic poetry of a land, a people, a frontier.
—MARTIN SCORSESE, film director

He's the only mathematical guitar genius I've ever run into who does not offend my intestinal nervousness with his rear-guard sound.   —BOB DYLAN, on Robbie Robertson

I think the fact that Patti Smith was the first really frank woman was what made her so strong. She wasn't afraid of being ugly—and I don't mean physically—she allowed herself to be ugly, to sound ugly and to say ugly things and she did so in a very feminine way.
—TANYA DONELLY, of Belly, 1994

It was neat that I got to see [Bob] Dylan, got to spend time with him before I did my record. Even though we never discussed the record. . . . We never discussed nothing. We never talked. . . . You know how I felt? I been talking to him in my brain for twelve years, and now I don't have nothing to say to him. I feel like we should have telepathy by now.   —PATTI SMITH, 1976

Bob Dylan is the closest thing to a saint that I know of among white people in America.   —NINA SIMONE

Can you imagine what a world it would be if we didn't have a Bob Dylan? It would be awful.   —GEORGE HARRISON, 1992

We saw this scruffy little pale-faced dirty human being get up in front of the crowd and start singing his "Song to Woody." I, of course, internally went to shreds, 'cause it was so beautiful.

—JOAN BAEZ, recalling the first time she saw
Bob Dylan perform, 1983

A strong recurring feeling I get from watching Dylan perform is the sense of him playing for Big Stakes. He says he's "just a musician," and in his boots he needs that kind of protection from intellectual probes, which are a constant threat to any artist. Even so, the repercussions of his art don't have to be answered by him at all. They fall on us as questions and that's where they belong.

—SAM SHEPARD, playwright and actor,
Rolling Thunder Logbook

You don't have to hear what Bob Dylan's saying, you just have to hear the way he says it. —JOHN LENNON (1940–1980), 1970

I said [to Dylan], "Those songs are gonna last forever, Bob." And he said, "Your songs are gonna last forever too—the only thing is, no one's gonna be able to play them."

—BONO

Art is sincere. Somehow you can tell the difference when a song is written just to get on the radio and when what someone does is their whole life. That comes through in [Bob] Dylan, Paul Simon, Willie Nelson. There is no separating their life from their music.

—LYLE LOVETT, 1995

Bob freed your mind the way Elvis freed your body.

—BRUCE SPRINGSTEEN,
on Bob Dylan, 1988

If you live in New Jersey and don't love Springsteen, they raise your taxes. —JON BON JOVI, 1988

Bruce Springsteen sings about Americans—blue-collar Americans trapped and suffocating in old broken-down small towns. His songs are about working-class people, desperate people hanging on to the American dream by a thread. . . . He touches his fans and they touch him. His shows are like old-time revivals with the same old-time message: If they work hard enough and long enough, like Springsteen himself, they can also make it to the promised land.

—BERNARD GOLDBERG,
CBS correspondent

James [Taylor] is a dreamer. He dreams a lot about where he's not, doing things he isn't doing, seeing things he hasn't seen.

—CARLY SIMON

[Joni Mitchell], more than I, I think, has a need for creativity, for her art. More of a need to relieve herself, to satisfy herself, than almost anyone else I've ever met.

—JAMES TAYLOR

She's a living Barbie doll but a little bit on the blue side.

—JONI MITCHELL, on Madonna, 1991

[She's] the kind of woman who comes into your room at 3 A.M. and sucks your life out.

—MILO MILES, music editor,
describing Madonna

Not everybody is open to Van Morrison, so they'd have to get their information from Janet Jackson or Madonna. Pop music has just as much a function as anything else.

—SINÉAD O'CONNOR, 1992

I was considering doing a song with Billy Idol. That would have been good because we're both white and plastic and blond.

—MADONNA

He's probably the most eclectic artist I've seen since me.
—DAVID BOWIE, on Prince, 1987

Prince is a total master of the stage—he's totally in control. And he's so fucking funky. —JULIANA HATFIELD, 1995

If it hadn't been for Elvis, I'd probably be driving a snowplow in Minneapolis. —PRINCE

Hearing [Elvis Presley] for the first time was like busting out of jail. —BOB DYLAN

This cat came out in red pants and a green coat and a pink shirt and socks, and he had this sneer on his face and he stood behind the mike for five minutes, I'll bet, before he made a move. Then he hit his guitar lick, and he broke two strings. I'd been playing for ten years, and I hadn't broken a total of two strings. So there he was, these two strings dangling, and he hadn't done anything yet, and these high school girls were screaming and fainting and running up to the stage, and then he started to move his hips real slow like he had a thing for his guitar. That was Elvis Presley when he was about 19. . . . He made chills run up my back, man, like when your hair starts grabbing at your collar.

—BOB LUMAN, country singer, on the first
time he saw Elvis perform

The man never had a bad take. One was better than the other. He was like an Olympic champion. He could sing all day.

—JERRY LEIBER, songwriter of Elvis classics
such as "Jailhouse Rock," on Elvis Presley

[Elvis Presley] was a man's man. A mama's boy. A native genius of the spirit. A tentative step above white trash. A vain hick. A valiant hero. The maker of some of the finest gospel and spiritual records ever released. A sacrilegious church truant. A loyal friend. A loutish bully. An archetypal southern gentleman. A low-living letch. A princely appreciator of his fans. A pasty-face pillhead. The rock voice without peer. The rock enigma without equal. The King.

—TIMOTHY WHITE, rock journalist and
biographer, *Rock Lives*

Before Elvis there was nothing.

—JOHN LENNON (1940–1980)

Elvis [Presley] was very androgynous. People in the older generation were afraid of Elvis because of this. . . . I saw Elvis as a rock singer, and obviously you were attracted to him because he was a good-looking guy. But they saw an effeminate guy. I mean, if you look at the pictures, the eyes are done with makeup, and everything's perfect.   —MICK JAGGER, 1994

We love this [roots music] stuff because it's really good music and it comes from people who are really sincere about it. When people start making fun about Elvis and forget all he did to change the world and just concentrate on the fact that he got all fat and wore a white jumpsuit, it's really sad and shallow.

—LUX, of the Cramps, 1995

Without Elvis, none of us could have made it.

—BUDDY HOLLY (1936–1959)

[Buddy Holly] scored with a dazzling series of firsts during an era when everyone followed the flock. He was one of the first white rock stars to rely almost exclusively on his own material. The Crickets were probably the first white group to feature the lead-rhythm-bass-drums lineup. He was the first rock singer to double-track his voice and guitar. He was the first to use strings on a rock 'n' roll record. In addition, he popularized the Fender Stratocaster and was probably the only rock star to wear glasses onstage!

—MALCOLM JONES, music journalist

I just carry that other time around with me. . . . The music of the late '50s and early '60s when music was at that root level—that for me is meaningful music. The singers and musicians I grew up with transcend nostalgia—Buddy Holly and Johnny Ace are just as valid to me today as then.   —BOB DYLAN

For myself, no one has been more of an inspiration than Elton John. When I first heard "Bennie and the Jets," I knew I had to be a performer.   —AXL ROSE, of Guns N' Roses, 1994

I truly loved that man. He would come to the house, so polite and gentle. And so handsome. Wow! As much as anybody, Sam made me want to sing. He would just say "Sing, girl." And believe me, that was enough. —ARETHA FRANKLIN, on Sam Cooke

When I first saw this man and heard him, I said, "Oh my God! Look at him!" This man was so smooth, so good and such class. . . . You gotta understand: a pretty boy that's got class! I mean, I've seen women just pass out wanting to get to him!

—SAM MOORE, of Sam and Dave, on Sam Cooke

I was hanging out with this guy who was in a motorcycle club. One day while visiting their "clubhouse," he took me into his room and bolted the door shut. He wanted to play me his favorite record, but he didn't want any of his "brothers" to hear it. . . . It was Sam Cooke singing "The Great Pretender." I looked at this white supremacist lowlife, with his hand on his heart and his eyes shut, swaying to that clear, black voice, and I thought, "I'll have some of that."

—CHRISSIE HYNDE, of the Pretenders, on how her band got their name

Anything Sam Cooke did I would do . . . apart from getting shot in a hotel room by a hooker. —ROD STEWART, 1995

A lot of times when he was singing onstage, we'd just get mesmerized and even miss cues. I'd get goose bumps and think, "This man is incredible." —SHEILA E., on playing with Marvin Gaye

What artist in his right mind wouldn't be intimidated by Stevie Wonder?
—MARVIN GAYE (1939–1984), 1979

I sat in on some Stevie Wonder sessions, and Stevie would sit there and sing "da da da da" and then fill in the words. I said, "Wait a minute, you mean all I gotta do is fill in the da da's?" When I found that out, the ball game was over.

—LIONEL RICHIE, 1983

I think Garth Brooks is really good. . . . The one thing about country music is that it tells great stories. You know who wants to do a country album? Stevie Wonder!

—STEVIE WONDER, 1995

Etta [James]. What a voice, I love that woman's voice, I'd kill for that voice.

—BRIAN JOHNSON, of AC/DC, 1995

Sylvester Stewart, he's a poet. And then there's also Sly Stone, the street cat, the hustler, the pimp, the conniver, sly as a fox and cold as a stone. . . . That's the street strutter, the street dude who walks up there with that charisma that holds an audience captive, right? . . . He's irresponsible, opportunistic and unethical, and he pimps our minds if we let him.

—DAVID KAPRALIK, personal manager of
Sylvester Stewart, a.k.a. Sly Stone, 1971

Before I heard them, I was planning to be a mechanical draftsman. But P-Funk's music opened my mind up to the idea that there are no barriers except the ones you believe in. They were rebels who broke all the rules. Their sound was real eerie and radical as hell. It had so much flavor.

—DR. DRE, on '70s funk master George Clinton
and his band, P-Funk, 1995

I'd like to be inducted [into the Rock 'n' Roll Hall of Fame] by Jimmy Page or Jerry Lee Lewis. I would want him to say, like, two words, then vomit from drinking too much. That would be more of a statement about rock 'n' roll than anything.

—DEAN WEAN, of Wean, 1995

John and I told him, "Turn around so they can see you; make a fuss." So the next night he carried on, stood up, kicked the stool back, and a new Jerry Lee was born.

—CARL PERKINS, recalling advice he gave to
shy newcomer Jerry Lee Lewis, who was touring
with Perkins and Johnny Cash

He'll burn a goddamn piano if he has to.

—WAYLON JENNINGS, on Jerry Lee Lewis's
ability to drive an audience wild

I want to be the Jerry Fucking Lee Lewis of our time.

—TERENCE TRENT D'ARBY

I want to be a Frank Sinatra figure. And I will succeed.

—DAVID BOWIE, 1976

[He's] the only genius in the business.

—FRANK SINATRA'S assessment of
Ray Charles

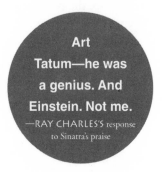

Art Tatum—he was a genius. And Einstein. Not me.

—RAY CHARLES'S response
to Sinatra's praise

I was listening to B. B. King, Ray Charles, and those guys, trying to figure out how to do it. Listening to those people—how they played so well and so relaxed—I'm still trying to learn to play that way. I probably will be for the rest of my life.

—STEVIE RAY VAUGHN (1954–1990)

His spirit is with us here. You can take all the meat, the bones, the dust—whatever's left—and it don't mean a whole lot. But the music is what he loved and where the spirit came, and we've got that. That way he's always with us.

—DR. JOHN, on Stevie Ray Vaughn, 1995

I don't think there's anybody that tears into a song the way [Stevie Ray Vaughn] did. I think Stevie Ray was coming from someplace so deep that there's nobody you can compare him to.

—BONNIE RAITT, 1995

I hadn't heard him play in a couple of years. He just walked onstage and started playing like he'd been doing it forever. Last time I saw him, it's like he was still struggling with it, you know? But he stood up there and smoked that first night in Austin. At that moment, I knew he was gonna be famous.

—JIMMIE VAUGHN, on seeing his brother,
Stevie Ray Vaughn, perform for the first time in
Austin, Texas

Jimmie makes love to you the way he plays, but Stevie just throws you down and rapes you.

—EDDIE STOUT, Austin musician, explaining
the difference between Jimmie Vaughn's and
Stevie Ray Vaughn's guitar styles

I felt so much love for him. I felt like he was my father and I was his adopted son. It was honor bound. But I was in love with Muddy before I ever met him.

—ERIC CLAPTON, on his mentor,
Muddy Waters, 1983

When I heard him, I realized the connection between all the music I'd heard. He made it all explainable. He was like the code book.

—KEITH RICHARDS,
on Muddy Waters, 1983

You know, people talk about T. S. Eliot, Ezra Pound, William Carlos Williams, and Robert Frost as the great American poets—and they are. But for me, Muddy Waters and his peers and the great black jazz artists are the true poets of America. They sacrificed everything for their music, and they always kept their style and their dignity in times when it was very hard to do.

—PETER WOLF, of J. Geils Band, 1983

I think they should put up a statue like the one in Thailand of the Buddha. You know, the ones that are 50 feet high, and he's sitting there with a beatific smile on his face and his eyes closed? I think they should do one of those of Muddy in Chicago.

—BONNIE RAITT, on Muddy Waters, 1983

I've looked up to David Bowie all my life, but now I think he should look up to us.

—IAN McCULLOCH, of Echo &
the Bunnymen

John Lennon once said to me, "Look, it's very simple—say what you mean, make it rhyme, and put a backbeat to it." And he was right: "Instant karma's gonna get you," boom. I keep comin' back to that these days. He was tight, man. There is no more than that. There is no more.
—DAVID BOWIE, 1983

If it wasn't for John Lennon, a lot of us would be someplace much different tonight. It's a hard world that asks you to live a lot of things that are unlivable. And it's hard to come out here and play tonight.
—BRUCE SPRINGSTEEN, in concert soon
after learning about John Lennon's
assassination, 1980

The thing was we meet and shake hands and say great—them dude they nice. I really like meet them and sit down and chat with them. They're bredrens. Jah just love roots. Them guys are roots. Them guys are all right, ya know.
—BOB MARLEY (1945–1981), on meeting the
Beatles, 1975

I don't think there's a single song that I've written in my entire life that doesn't have little pieces of something the Beatles once did.
—ROBIN WILSON, of Gin Blossoms, 1995

The Beatles are as embedded in contemporary modern music as any classical composer would have been in his time.
—BOB MOULD, of Hüsker Dü, 1995

The closest Western civilization has come to unity since the Congress of Vienna in 1815 was the week the *Sgt. Pepper* album was released. In every city in Europe and America the stereo systems and the radio played, "What would you think if I sang out of tune . . . Woke up, got out of bed . . . looked much older, and the bag across her shoulder . . . in the sky with diamonds, Lucy in the . . ." and everyone listened. At the time I happened to be driving across the country on Interstate 80. In each city where I stopped for gas or food—Laramie, Ogalla, Moline, South Bend—the melodies wafted in from some far-off transistor radio or portable hi-fi. It was the most amazing thing I'd ever heard. For a brief while the irreparably fragmented consciousness of the West was unified, at least in the minds of the young.
—LANGDON WINNER, author, 1968

The Beatles, who like many of the new groups write their own music, have added interesting embellishments—counter points, madrigal effects, tonal progressions, which are so adroitly done that musicologists openly wonder if the British lads know what on earth they are doing.

—*Life* magazine, 1965

They were doing things nobody was doing. Their chords were outrageous, just outrageous, and their harmonies made it all valid. . . . But I kept it to myself that I really dug them. Everybody thought they were for the teenyboppers, that they were going to pass right away. But it was obvious to me that they had staying power. I knew they were pointing the direction where music had to go. . . . In my head, the Beatles were it.

—BOB DYLAN, 1971

But it's a little galling now to find that I own less of "Yesterday" than Michael Jackson! It's a thorn in my side, and I keep thinking I should phone him up. I don't hold a grudge, but if you're listening, Michael, I'll have "Yesterday" and "Here, There and Everywhere" back—just for a laugh—and a couple of others.

—PAUL McCARTNEY; Michael Jackson
owns the rights to the Beatles' catalogue of
songs; 1987

[Michael Jackson] kind of idolized me, and he wanted to sing like me . . . everything; people couldn't tell which was me and which was Michael.

—DIANA ROSS

I'll never forget the day I was walking the halls at the Ed Sullivan Theater. I walked past his dressing room. . . . And he calls me in, and he says he saw our rehearsal that day, and said, "No matter what you do, never forget to thank God for your talent." He looked me in the eyes. He was unique, he was really kind. Such a nice man.

—MICHAEL JACKSON,
on Ed Sullivan, 1989

There's only one Who drummer. Just one—Keith Moon.

—ROGER DALTRY, 1976

Artie [Garfunkel] was always the best singer.

—PAUL SIMON, 1975

Alice Cooper helped my life because he was my first hero.

—JOEY RAMONE, of the Ramones, 1979

At the end of the show, of course, he pulled out his penis. He'd been singing about it the whole night and I was just thinking "Let's see it." And there it was. —JIM KERR, of Simple Minds, on attending an Iggy Pop concert, 1995

I never felt I was a great performer. To me, Iggy Pop's a great performer. —RIC OCASEK, of the Cars, 1991

Chuck Berry was the ultimate performer. If you look at his lyrics, as far as I'm concerned, he's Shakespeare. In fact, to me, he's bigger than Shakespeare. —BRIAN JOHNSON, of AC/DC, 1995

Domino, he was creative. No matter what he does [his own sound] comes through. He could be singing the national anthem, you'd still know by the time he said two words it was him, obviously, unmistakably, and pleasurably him.

—COSIMO MATASSA, studio owner and originator of the New Orleans sound, on Fats Domino

Sonny affected the girls like an aphrodisiac. When he bent over the mike and leaned to one side, sensuously gyrating his shoulders and caressing the air with his hands, the girls would shriek, "Ride my alley, Sonny! Ride my alley!" —JACK SCHIFFMAN, *Uptown: The Story of Harlem's Apollo Theatre*, on Sonny Til, lead singer of the Orioles

My personal opinion is, the '70s is when the best music was made. Some motherfuckers had orchestras! Had string sections and they'd have to sit there and orchestrate a song. And put some vocals to it. . . . Curtis Mayfield, that motherfucker was bad as shit. Isaac Hayes, Barry White, y'knowhumsayin'? Them brothers was in there *doing* it. —DR. DRE, 1996

I asked, "Tori, what kind of guitar sound do you want here," and I swear she said, "An unshaven Moroccan yogurt spice." I said, "Okay—that's just what I was planning on doing."

—DAVE NAVARRO, of Red Hot Chili
Peppers, on the unique experience of recording
with Tori Amos

She's one of the first women performers I worked with who has got the same aggressive thing that I've got. A lot of women performers are quite static—or certainly were in the '60s. . . . They weren't like Tina. She was like a female version of Little Richard and would respond to the audience—really go out and grab them.

—MICK JAGGER, on Tina Turner, 1994

Courtney [Love] has that element of danger. You never know what she's going to do next. We're not used to seeing that in a woman. We're used to seeing that from Jim Morrison, or Iggy Pop, or from Johnny Rotten in the early days of the Sex Pistols. She's a rock star in the sort of unpredictable, volatile way that people voyeuristically expect.

—LISA ROBINSON, journalist, 1995

She was so symbolic of a lot of women in America with bad self-image problems, and that meant her voice had this incredible vulnerability to it, in the midst of all that really schlocky music. In retrospect, in relation to her life, her lyrics were tragically profound.

—KIM GORDON, of Sonic Youth, on Karen
Carpenter, 1994

Musically, I dig Led Zeppelin, but vocally, I've never been influenced much in the Robert Plant direction because the dungeons-and-dragons-esque lyrics never really did much for me. Besides, you'd need a pair of pliers to get me to be able to sing in that range.

—SCOTT WEILAND,
of Stone Temple Pilots, 1995

All the great bands were live bands. James Brown, ZZ Top, Led Zep, Jane's Addiction.

—HENRY ROLLINS, 1995

I owe a lot of who I am and what I've been and what I've done to the beatniks from the '50s and to the poetry and art and music that I've come in contact with. I feel like I'm part of a continuous line of a certain thing in American culture, of a root.

—JERRY GARCIA (1942–1995), of the
Grateful Dead

Joseph Campbell labeled me a conjurer one night. He was watching us play and said, "What you are is a conjurer." I thought about it for a coupla months and decided, "Yeah, you're right."

—BOB WEIR, of the Grateful Dead, 1989

One [book] I read in college that's still a favorite is *Jude the Obscure* by Thomas Hardy. There are two women in the book who are total opposites, one very earthy and lusty, the other very pristine and spiritual. And this man is torn between these two extremes—which is what a lot of my own writing is about. I also love *Walden, or Life in the Woods,* and anything else by Thoreau. And Mark Twain. And Ralph Waldo Emerson's essays. Emerson's essay on self-reliance was literally where I got the nerve to become a songwriter.

—DON HENLEY, 1990

When I hear the Beach Boys I think of getting tanned and surfin' and summer love and all that crap, but when I hear the Four Seasons belting "Rag Doll" or "Dawn, go away I'm no good for you," man, I picture smokestacks, dirty streets, tenements in the Bronx, and poor, tough kids that are survivors.

—BRUCE "COUSIN BRUCIE" MORROW,
New York disc jockey, on what he likes about
the sound of the Four Seasons

In 1985 you had the stigma of Mötley Crüe and Ratt. Today people think metal's dead. But the biggest band in the world is metal, and I'm not talking about Hootie and the Blowfish. I'm talking about Metallica.

—SCOTT IAN, of Anthrax, 1995

weasels ripped my flesh

Joe Strummer is a fake. That only puts him in there with Dylan and Jagger and Townshend and most of the other great rock writers, because almost all of them in one way or another were fakes. Townshend has a middle-class education. Lou Reed went to Syracuse University before matriculating to the sidewalks of New York. Dylan faked his whole career; the only difference was that he used to be good at it and now he sucks.

—LESTER BANGS (1949–1982), music critic and journalist, *Psychotic Reactions and Carburetor Dung*

The Beatles were elevator music in my lifetime.

—MICHAEL STIPE, of R.E.M., 1992

The Beatles are not merely awful; they are so unbelievably horrible, so appallingly unmusical, so dogmatically insensitive to the magic of the art, that they qualify as crowned heads of anti-music.

—WILLIAM F. BUCKLEY, JR., conservative journalist and political commentator

The Beatles are a passing phase. They are the symptoms of the uncertainties of the times. I hope, when they get older, they'll get a haircut.

—BILLY GRAHAM, evangelist

[The Beatles] were just a band that made it very, very big, that's all.

—JOHN LENNON (1940–1980), 1971

It hurt me. Deep.

—PAUL McCARTNEY, responding to John
Lennon's dismissive remarks about the Beatles

I think it's a lot of hype. I like "Honky Tonk Women," but I think Mick's a joke with all that fag dancing.

—JOHN LENNON (1940–1980), on the
Rolling Stones, 1971

Mick Jagger has child-bearing lips.

—JOAN RIVERS

Mick Jagger is a scared little boy who is about as sexy as a pissing toad. He moves like a parody between a majorette girl and Fred Astaire.

—TRUMAN CAPOTE (1924–1984)

Dylan once told Keith [Richards], "I could have written 'Satisfaction,' but you couldn't have written 'Tambourine Man.' " That's true, but could he sing it?

—MICK JAGGER, on Bob Dylan, 1968

If you're the singer of the band, you always get more attention than anyone else. Brian [Jones] got very jealous when I got attention. And the main jealousy was because Keith [Richards] and I started writing songs, and he wasn't involved in that. To be honest, Brian had no talent for writing songs. None. I've never known a guy with less talent for songwriting.

—MICK JAGGER; Rollingstones' onetime
guitarist Brian Jones overdosed and drowned in
his swimming pool in 1969; 1994

You better ask the bitch.

—KEITH RICHARDS, when asked if there will
be an end to the bitching between himself and
Mick Jagger, 1987

I promise you they'll never be back on our show.

—ED SULLIVAN (1901–1974), after the
Rolling Stones' infamous appearance on his
show, 1964

I don't like the Who much.

—PETE TOWNSHEND, 1994

In his own admittance, he's a compulsive liar. He changes his mind an awful lot. It's not important what he says.

—ROGER DALTRY, on Pete Townshend, 1994

I think [Pete] Townshend's always wanted to be me.

—ROGER DALTRY

For me, it's that fear of becoming an oldies band. I saw it happen to the Rolling Stones, the Who. They're doing all the hits to keep paying the mortgages. That's death. That's the way to kill your band.

—PETER BUCK, of R.E.M.

The Who and the Stones are revolting. All they're good for is making money.

—JOHNNY ROTTEN, of the Sex Pistols

The Sex Pistols were a fiasco. A farce.

—JOHNNY ROTTEN,
of the Sex Pistols, 1980

John's just jealous because I'm the brains of the group. I've written all the songs, even from the beginning when I wasn't in the group. They were so useless, they had to come to me because they couldn't think of anything by themselves.

—SID VICIOUS (1957–1979), on Johnny
Rotten and the Sex Pistols

Just a mindless twerp.

—DAVID BOWIE, on Sid Vicious, 1987

The Sex Pistols are like some contagious disease.
—MALCOLM McLAREN, Sex Pistols' manager

They're going to be the ones responsible for this corporate, alternative and cock-rock fusion.

—KURT COBAIN (1967–1994), of Nirvana,
on fellow Seattle rockers Pearl Jam, 1992

She's getting the success, but, okay, she's getting her teeth capped, another nose job, more body work. Is that somebody who likes herself? I don't think so. I think that's somebody who can't stand herself.

That's a success in the most conventional American terms. I'm not interested in conventionality at all. What happened to women paving the way? Do we need a female Axl Rose? I don't think so.

—KIM GORDON, of Sonic Youth, on Courtney Love, 1995

Let's face it, Alanis Morissette is like a tame Courtney Love. What is Alanis Morissette being held up as? This feministic step forward. The fact is, it's people like Courtney and Kat Bjelland [from Babes in Toyland] who carved out that road. We should be rewarding the real artists.

—BILLY CORGAN, of the Smashing Pumpkins, 1995

Yeah, I fucked Reznor, but it wasn't that great of an experience. I was slumming.

—COURTNEY LOVE, of Hole, on Trent Reznor of Nine Inch Nails, 1995

Oh, she was horrible. She was always super-competitive and threatened by me.

—JONI MITCHELL, on Joan Baez, 1991

I couldn't get into the '50s rock at all—didn't like it. I'll never forget, a girlfriend called me up one night and said, "You ought to see this guy on television named Elvis Presley. He's great." Well, I turned on our set and saw this greaser sliding all over the screen who made me sick.

—GRACE SLICK, of Jefferson Airplane

His kind of music is deplorable, a rancid smelling aphrodisiac.

—FRANK SINATRA, on Elvis Presley, 1956

Ozzy Osbourne, God bless him, will always be Ozzy Osbourne and he can't be anything else, even though he's over 40 years old. He's still pouring himself into tight satin trousers, biting the heads off chickens, wears girls' clothes and has flowing locks. It's very hard for him to get out of that.   —STING, 1987

You could tell the moment when the Police stopped touring—they went from being a hot club band to being an art project.
—MIKE MILLS, of R.E.M.

The Smiths are more important than the Police! We're more important than they ever were, or ever will be.
—JOHNNY MARR, of the Smiths, 1984

Madonna is closer to organized prostitution than anything else.
—MORRISSEY, of the Smiths

I'm irritated that the world we live in, and its culture and society, can build and maintain Madonna.
—NATALIE MERCHANT, 1989

Comparing Madonna with Marilyn Monroe is like comparing Raquel Welch with the back of a bus.
—BOY GEORGE

Boy George makes me sick.   —MADONNA

I always gave the Beach Boys a good song to sing—and now I find myself totally disillusioned with the Beach Boys. The Beach Boys left me to figure out all there was to figure out with records and with people. They left me with this feeling inside of "You better get another album out or we'll kill ya!" Although we stay together as a group, as people we're a far cry from friends.
—BRIAN WILSON, of the Beach Boys, 1988

All I could think about her was B.O.—she wouldn't be bad-looking if she would wash up and glue herself together a little bit.
—ANDY WARHOL (1928–1987),
on Patti Smith

Groups like Genesis and Yes are about as exciting as used Kleenex.

—NICK LOWE

Somebody has to react against Hootie and the Blowfish.

—BEN WATT, of Everything But the Girl, 1997

Led Zeppelin is just a bunch of stupid idiots who wrote cool riffs.

—CHRIS CORNELL, of Soundgarden

I'm actually quite a decent chap, and the rest of the group are wankers.

—JOOLS HOLLAND, of Squeeze

In Fleetwood Mac, I was pretty much told to be quiet at all times. I was so intimidated because I didn't feel like anybody really wanted me to be in that band and that they only wanted Lindsey [Buckingham] and me along for the ride.

—STEVIE NICKS, 1995

A lot of Michael's success is due to timing and luck. It could just as easily have been me.

—JERMAINE JACKSON, on brother Michael Jackson

We had this group which we all knew had the potential to be something really big, and Jim [Morrison] was trying to sabotage it by fucking up at every turn. We would call a rehearsal, Jim wouldn't show, and we'd get a call from Blythe, Arizona, telling us that he was in jail.

—ROBBY KRIEGER, of the Doors, 1994

Jerry and I would fight like cats and dogs—over syllables, or a note, or a phrase. It never came to the blows, but it could get rough.

—MIKE STOLLER, on his writing partner, Jerry Leiber; Leiber and Stoller were responsible for writing dozens of early rock 'n' roll and Motown hits, including "Hound Dog" and "Yakety Yak"

On a personal level, I have nothing against Dave Gilmour further-
ing his own goals. It's just the idea of Dave's solo career masquerad-
ing as Pink Floyd that offends me!

—ROGER WATERS, on the legal battle
concerning Gilmour's continued use of the
name Pink Floyd after Waters left
the band, 1988

I don't share Roger's sense of angst about music, and the world. . . .
Granted, I did less work with Pink Floyd back in the old days, but
that was something Roger was forcing. And now the poor chap has
lost his whip hand. —DAVE GILMOUR, of Pink Floyd, 1988

He was the Pat Boone of rap. —JELLO BIAFRA, of Dead Kennedys, on
Vanilla Ice, 1996

When I listen to the radio I think, "We ought to be on here and this
shit shouldn't be." Because face it, no one needs to hear Jethro Tull
on the radio anymore. . . . They're still playing the worst shit of the
'70s and calling that classic rock. Boy, if "Aqualung" is a classic,
then fucking "I'll Be You" [a Replacements' song] is *history.*

—TOMMY STINSON,
of the Replacements, 1989

We've never been darlings of the press. In fact, I remember reading
one article that said we were the only band that was uglier than Los
Lobos. So I went and checked out the movie *La Bamba,* and saw
Los Lobos at the end, and I said, "Huh-uh, no way." People may
think we're ugly, but we're not that ugly.

—MIKE MUIR, of Suicidal Tendencies

When we go home, we don't hang out together. I like to have pic-
nics, drink beer, go bowling, be outside. If we saw each other at a
bar, we'd say hi, but we wouldn't sit at the same table.

—EMILY SALIERS, of Indigo Girls, on fellow
Indigo Girl Amy Ray, 1989

Troubled Genius

<u>you can't always</u>
<u>get what you want</u>

aybe my audiences can enjoy my music more if they think I'm destroying myself.

—JANIS JOPLIN (1943–1970), 1969

If some people had their way, they'd just want me to weep and suffer for them for the rest of my life, because people live vicariously through their artists. —JONI MITCHELL

Great artists suffer for the people.

—MARVIN GAYE (1939–1984)

We can't be inspired all the time, can we? And those of us who are made to feel that we have to be, grow weary and even ill from the stress of the crazy, unfair responsibility put on us.

—STEVE WINWOOD, 1989

Until I realized that rock music was my connection to the rest of the human race, I felt like I was dying, for some reason, and I didn't really know why. —BRUCE SPRINGSTEEN

It's false to think that musicians and artists have to suffer for their work. It's a myth. I want to hear from someone who's fulfilled.

—TORI AMOS, 1994

We never really fit in with those artist types who sit around and smoke cigarettes and talk about music and wear leather and stuff. I guess that's what set us apart. We weren't depressed.

—JIM SONEFELD, of Hootie and the
Blowfish, 1995

Since our music is so depressing, everybody expects us to run around in black and whine about shit. But that's such a misconception. We just get together and fuck around. We're like the Monkees or something.
—SEAN KINNEY, of Alice in Chains, 1996

I've always enjoyed myself. Unhappy periods for me last about twenty minutes.
—KEITH MOON (1946–1978), of the Who

I don't have the blues, so I don't play the blues. I'm a pretty happy guy.
—EDDIE VAN HALEN

Everybody has the blues—that's what it comes down to.
—JAMES TAYLOR

It's not like I'm dwelling on the negative. If my life was all sunshine, that's what I'd write about. I'm attracted more to the bad things because there are more of them, frankly.
—COURTNEY LOVE, of Hole, 1992

I don't know how people can write happy music. I like sad music, it makes me feel better, more alive I guess. I like tortured people.
—KAT BJELLAND, of Babes in Toyland, 1994

I just don't want to be boring. 'Cause if you're really happy, who wants to hear about it? Why do you want to tell anybody?
—LYLE LOVETT, 1992

Constant and repetitive fulfillment is not good for the human spirit. We all need rain and good old depression.

—MORRISSEY, 1995

I actually embrace the idea of being happy now. I've had my share of pain, and I probably will in the future, too. But I've gotta say, it's sculpted me into the person I am now.

—ANNIE LENNOX, 1983

When I look back, it seems like the guitarists who had a real effect on me were people who, in a sense, were very driven—maybe centered, or maybe tortured—but seeking souls, searching souls.

—STEVE VAI

I'm thought of as this pissy, complaining, freaked-out schizophrenic who wants to kill himself all the time.

—KURT COBAIN (1967–1994),
of Nirvana, 1994

The fact is, I can't fool you, any one of you. It simply isn't fair to you or me. The worst crime I can think of would be to pull people off by faking it and pretending as if I'm having a hundred percent fun. Sometimes I feel as though I should have a punch-in time clock before I walk out onstage. I've tried everything in my power to appreciate it, and I do. God, believe me, I do. But it's not enough. . . . I'm too much of an erratic, moody person, and I don't have the passion anymore, so remember—it's better to burn out than to fade away.

—KURT COBAIN (1967–1994), from his
suicide note, taped and read out loud by
Courtney Love for a gathering of
Nirvana fans, 1994

I'm really sorry, you guys. I don't know what I could have done. . . . Just tell [Cobain] he's a fucker, okay? Just say, "Fucker, you're a fucker," and that you love him.

—COURTNEY LOVE, her response after she'd
finished reading the note, 1994

[Brian Jones] was a very sad, pitiable figure at the end. He was a talented musician, but he let it go and proved to be a rather sad precursor to a lot of other people. Why this should be, I don't know. I find it rather morbid, but it does keep happening, with people like Kurt Cobain. Why? Does this happen in accounting, too? Is this something that happens in every profession, it's just that we don't read about the accountants?

—MICK JAGGER; Brian Jones, one-time guitarist for the Rolling Stones, died in 1969 by overdosing and drowning in his swimming pool; it's unclear whether it was an accident or suicide; 1994

I think most people in the entertainment industry are very insecure and fame is being loved, almost. It's being fulfilled. When you reach that pinnacle of success you find yourself as empty as you ever were, because nothing outside of yourself could ever make you feel whole. And that's when people put guns in their mouths or become drug addicts or whatever addiction they choose.

—BOY GEORGE, 1996

You devote your whole life to entertaining people who, in the end, depress you so much you off yourself.

—KRIS KRISTOFFERSON

I wouldn't kill myself . . . that's been done already. I think about it sometimes, though.

—DAVE PIRNER, of Soul Asylum, 1995

There was a time when things seemed desperate, and I thought taking my life might be a way out. I made a couple of really weak attempts, mostly just to see if I could do it, and I couldn't.

—LAYNE STALEY, of Alice in Chains, 1996

I thought I was used to everything. But yesterday it dawned on me that there's a possibility that I'm becoming . . . everything . . . I detest.

—BJÖRK, 1995

I never felt like a self-destructive sort of person when I started out. I admit I may have been the first performer to vent his immediate angers in this format—if I was pissed off, I sang about it. But that was only part of what I did.

—IGGY POP, 1986

I guess I'm just an emotionally disturbed character at heart. I've been on a blistering roller-coaster ride of mental-health ups and downs. . . . But for [the Chili Peppers], tragic and miraculous struggles are what it takes to make beautiful pieces of work. We haven't ever made any good music just being on an even keel.

—ANTHONY KIEDIS, of Red Hot Chili Peppers, 1995

My life is very turbulent emotionally . . . so I'm constantly in the state of having to figure out what's going on or what kind of thing I'm supposed to be getting from it or what I am meant to learn from a specific situation. Usually it's when something turbulent is going on that you have to work it out in your head and then get it onto a piece of paper, so you can look at it and say, "Yeah, that's how I feel."

—SINÉAD O'CONNOR, 1992

I've always put it down to emotional turmoil [that drives me to create]. That's more like a trigger; it sets off something that is actually dormant. It can be something that is triggered off by an outside stimulus like joy. A lot of people think it has to be from something particularly nasty or a problem of some kind, but it isn't necessary, I don't think. It's just something a little out of the ordinary in terms of mental stimulus, something that makes or breaks your day.

—ERIC CLAPTON, 1992

In ten years time I'll probably go mad. I do feel as if I'm going in that direction, because I'm a romantic and as such I'm basically fucked up. Yes, I should imagine that in ten years time I'll be completely insane.

—TERENCE TRENT D'ARBY

Madness might be attractive because we want to know the people who suffer from it a little bit more. We can learn from things that are not normal, and get a greater understanding from them.

—P. J. HARVEY, 1995

I tried therapy for a couple of months, but it was a waste of my money. It's like, knowing what the problem is doesn't solve the problem. They try to make you find reasons for things where there isn't always a reason. They sort of encourage you to blame people for things, but things just happen and that's just the way they are. I don't need no doctor to tell me it's okay to be angry. A doctor can't tell me things about myself that I don't already know.

—JULIANA HATFIELD, 1995

To compile all my therapy into one sentence: As a child I learned that it was more advantageous to be this creation than it was to be who I really am. But my personality is so strong that it kind of bubbled out from underneath, and it was tough to distinguish who was the faker and who was real.

—BILLY CORGAN, of the Smashing Pumpkins, 1994

I have a really hard time with people who present their resume of scars, I don't like it, it's really cheap.

—TANYA DONELLY, of Belly

There's nothing worse than a whiny musician. Make your work, stay committed to your work, stand by your work and shut up.

—TORI AMOS, 1995

Slacker, my ass. I mean, I never had any slack. I was working a $4-an-hour job trying to stay alive. I mean, that slacker kind of stuff is for people who have the time to be depressed about everything.

—BECK, 1994

Beck puts out that song "Loser," Kurt Cobain blows his face off, River Phoenix croaks from an OD in front of a club in Hollywood. I think it's a sign of the times to be way more self-destructive, way more apathetic.

—BILLIE JOE ARMSTRONG, of Green Day, 1995

It was a breeze in the '60s to grow up, compared to [the '90s]. The '60s were so open-ended. The dream was still there, the no-matter-what-you-could-make-it feeling. Kids today feel, "No matter what, I'm probably not going to make it."

—NEIL YOUNG, 1995

I used to be a really negative person in high school and college. I used to feel mad and miserable and depressed: I hate all this, I hate all that, or "God, I'm okay, why doesn't anybody like me?" Then I look back and see what's happened to the kids who were way popular, and I'm glad I wasn't ever popular in school.

—EDIE BRICKELL, 1989

Why was I raised to lose? Why wasn't I given the skills necessary to lead a successful, happy, productive, loving life? Why has it been impossible for me to maintain a relationship?

—BILLY CORGAN, of the Smashing Pumpkins

> **I get lonesome sometimes. I get lonesome right in the middle of a crowd.**
> —ELVIS PRESLEY (1935–1977)

I think that loneliness just very simply equals time, like if you have a lonely childhood . . . then you have a lot more time than someone who hasn't been lonely, and you have that much more time to work on yourself. . . . There's a lot more introspection and more reaching out and grabbing things from the outside world and pulling them in that goes on when you're lonely. You watch more.

—TANYA DONELLY, of Belly, 1994

He spends a lot of time, too much time, by himself. I try to get him out. . . . Michael has a lot of people around him, but he's very afraid. I don't know why. —DIANA ROSS, on Michael Jackson, 1972

My defenses were so great. The cocky rock 'n' roll hero who knows all the answers was actually a terrified guy who didn't know how to cry. —JOHN LENNON (1940–1980)

If I seem free it's because I'm always running.

—JIMI HENDRIX (1942–1970)

When the Police became successful, that meteoric rise coincided with a terrible ennui, a terrible sense of displacement. My first marriage was breaking up, my personal life was a mess. Just when you think everything is going fantastic, beneath it is this swamp.

—STING, 1991

I hear myself bitching about "it sucks to be popular," and I have to just stop because it's bullshit to say that. By the same token, I'm not more happy or content with my life than I was 10 years ago. I got everything I wanted in my life . . . except I don't really have a life now. I don't have any real friends, any relationships that mean anything to me, and I've turned myself into this music-creation-performance thing.

—TRENT REZNOR, of Nine Inch Nails, 1994

[The danger of fame is in] being completely empty but having all this popularity. Not feeling good inside, but having this mask on. . . . I'm up on the stage to entertain and play music, but that's not all there is to life. If I get stuck in this image deal, where I have been plenty of times before, I'm in trouble. 'Cause I forget who I am.

—STEVIE RAY VAUGHN (1954–1990)

I thought I couldn't handle this rock 'n' roll nonsense, and I just sat in my garden dribbling into the sound hole of my guitar, thinking, "Oh, well, looks like I'm going to be Mr. Casualty then." I went to psychiatrists and hypnotists, who'd get me to relive gigs. I'd be on the settee sweating profusely and shaking and all this stuff. . . . It took me at least a year to get over the shock and the physical rundown.

—ANDY PARTRIDGE, of XTC, on his nervous breakdown following XTC's first tour; the singer suffers from severe performance anxiety; 1989

I was touring with 'Til Tuesday, things were going well but we'd been on the road for months. I was getting incredibly exhausted; along with exhaustion comes this weird zombie-state. There was one particular moment where I remember getting out my Swiss army knife and trying to calculate where I could cut my hand—so it wouldn't permanently damage me but it would make it impossible to play, so I could get myself off the tour. I knew the promoters would come down on me, I knew the band would come down on me, and I knew that the record company would think I was a major-league asshole. . . . But I had my knife out and for a few seconds it didn't even enter my head that this would be an irrational, problematic solution. Then I suddenly see this picture of myself and I say, "Hold on. What am I thinking?"

—AIMEE MANN, 1996

When I first found out, back in '67, that my hearing was going, I was destroyed. I wanted to throw myself out a window. If I couldn't hear anymore—could you imagine—if I couldn't sing, what's the point in continuing? After all the work, hardship, all the sacrifices and waiting—not being able to sing? I mean, this is my life! And, I'll tell you, I decided at the time I did not want to live any longer. Period.

—FRANKIE VALLI, of the Four Seasons, 1977

There was not the kind of love for me in Los Angeles that I was accustomed to. I wanted more love, more respect for me as an artist. There were so many plots and plans against me. People were saying that I was finished. My personality took a horrible beating there. I couldn't work in that kind of psychological hell-hole. I won't go back until my tarnished image is repolished by my work.

—MARVIN GAYE (1939–1984), 1983

I'd like to have a little more internal peace. I'm sure everybody would.

—AXL ROSE, of Guns N' Roses, 1992

idon't even know why I do it sometimes.
Do I need more money? Do I need more platinum
and gold records? The only thing I can think of is
ego. —JOHN MELLENCAMP, 1994

The music is the central issue, and there are a number of periph-
eral issues that will pull you away from the music. One of them is
"Gee, I must be intelligent. . . ." Or, "Gosh, I'm powerful. . . ."
Or "Gee, I'm great. . . ." Or "I must be the sexiest thing on
earth. . . ." All of these are mistakes. They are all ways to misper-
ceive ourselves. What you are is incredibly lucky. You're a human
being, regular and normal, you put your pants on one leg at time,
same as everybody else. You've been given a gift, and if you understand you've been given a gift, you work very hard at it. You don't
abuse it.

—DAVID CROSBY, 1992

Yeah, I'm real spoiled. I've spoiled myself.

—AXL ROSE, of Guns N' Roses

I could be unbelievably horrible and stupid. On tours, I'd get on a
plane, then get off it, maybe six or eight times. I'd walk out of a
hotel suite because I didn't like the color of the bedspread. I
remember looking out of my room at the Inn on the Park one day
and saying, "It's too windy. Can someone please do something
about it?"

—ELTON JOHN

The problem is, you're catapulted into this position where your ego is blown up to the size of a major planet. And you begin to believe that you can do anything.   —MICHAEL STIPE, of R.E.M., 1992

My ego is already inflated way past the exploding stage.
                              —KURT COBAIN (1967–1994), of Nirvana

What comes out that surprises me is that most people see me as arrogant. To a certain extent, I am, but any artist worth his salt has arrogance. It's a prerequisite of being stage-worthy.
                              —STING, 1983

My reputation as a tyrant, Svengali, asshole, there's truth in that. . . . I created something beyond the sum of its parts. Maybe I pushed people, maybe I was a dick . . . but it worked.
                              —BILLY CORGAN, of the Smashing
                              Pumpkins, 1994

Yes, if there is such a thing as [genius], I am one.
                              —JOHN LENNON (1940–1980), 1971

I think I'm a genius. Point fucking blank.
                              —TERENCE TRENT D'ARBY

I . . . question the artistic ego, whether or not an artist should be allowed to vent his opinions. Because we're not cut out for that job. I mean, that's probably one of the reasons I didn't ever really want to be a singer, because it would probably place me in a position where I could give forth opinions, which I didn't really have the right to give. And, you know, I've been in situations where I had to take back what I've said. Many times. 'Cause I've mouthed off.
                              —ERIC CLAPTON, 1992

All I want to do is make those records and not have to think about the people who listen to them. So we don't. I don't know who listens to the records anyway. I don't really care what they think. 'Cause I know what I think and I know that I'm right.
                              —PETER BUCK, of R.E.M., 1988

Those radio people know who I am. And I know who I am. I don't need their confirmation. I don't cease to exist if they don't play my fucking records. —ELVIS COSTELLO

I sold more records than Elvis. Not after his death. But when I was the queen of rock 'n' roll, I sold more than he did when he was the king of rock 'n' roll. —JONI MITCHELL, 1991

If it was 1965, and we'd just put out our second album, we'd absolutely be the pop kings of the world. It would've been the Beatles, the Rolling Stones, Oasis, and then the Who. I firmly believe that. —NOEL GALLAGHER, of Oasis, 1997

I'm the real king of rock 'n' roll. I was singing rock before anybody knew what rock was, back when swing music was the big thing. People like Elvis Presley were the builders of rock 'n' roll—but I was the architect. —LITTLE RICHARD

When we were kids, everyone wanted to be in the Beatles. Now we are! I'm only kidding! THAT'S A JOKE!

—BONO

Everyone slags us off for comparing ourselves to great groups, but that's bullshit. I mean, they said that to the Beatles, as well.

—LARRY MULLEN, of U2, 1989

I am the Nureyev of rock 'n' roll.

—MEAT LOAF

I could never feel lonely because I love me. I think I'm dope, personally. I don't think there's nobody fresher than me. I am my fan. I'm my own dick. —KRS-ONE

Barry White's three best qualities are his love for music, his love for people, and his love for himself.

—BARRY WHITE

Currently, I don't listen to what anybody else is doing in music because there are so many things that seem to remind me a bit of what I do or have done. It gets incestuous. At the end of the day, you just have to know that no one can be you, and at best there can only be superficial similarities. I'm just getting further and further into myself. —BRYAN FERRY, of Roxy Music, 1985

Down in D.C. they talking about the go-go but I had them kids out in the streets while they were still babies, doing the popcorn with the Original Disco Man. Funk I invented back in the '50s. The rap thing I had down on my "Brother Rapp (Part I)," and you can check that. . . . Michael Jackson, he used to watch me from the wings and got his moon walk from my camel walk—he'll tell you that if you ask. Same way, I was slippin' and slidin' before Prince was out of his crib. . . . I ain't jealous, I'm zealous. I ain't teased, I'm pleased. Who's gonna do James Brown better'n James Brown? Think! —JAMES BROWN, 1986

I never considered myself the greatest, but I'm the best.
—JERRY LEE LEWIS

Let's face it, I'm a showoff.
—PETER FRAMPTON

If I weren't as talented as I am ambitious, I would be a gross monstrosity. —MADONNA

I'm the biggest singer in America. I'm the biggest singer in the world! —JANIS JOPLIN (1943–1970)

When do they give the award for the best ass?
—PRINCE, his acceptance speech after winning
Minnesota Musician of the Year, 1982

There are dozens of [female singers/songwriters], but I don't hear much there, frankly. When it comes to knowing where to put the chords, most of them can't touch me.

—JONI MITCHELL

I'm only interested in heavy metal when it's me who's playing it. I suppose it's a bit like smelling your own farts.

—JOHN ENTWISTLE, of the Who

I'm not afraid of anything at the moment. Actually, I'm afraid of two things: God and the IRS. That's it. You know, I get butterflies every time a record comes out. I'm, like, I hope people like it. I hope people buy it. But it's never no serious fear.

—DR. DRE, 1996

That people are always trying to provoke some kind of fight so they can sue me. I'm scared of thrashing an asshole and going to jail for it. For some reason I can walk into a room and someone will pick a fight. That's always happening with me.

—AXL ROSE, of Guns N' Roses, on what scares
him the most

I've always been a bitch. I'm no more a bitch now than when I was a rabid failure.

—SHIRLEY MANSON, of Garbage, 1997

Baby, I am a mean motherfucker. Don't you be writing nothin' nice 'cause you'd be jivin' people. I am the wicked. Dig? I am named the wicked, I got to be the wicked.

—WILSON PICKETT

You scared of me? You should be. Why do you think they call me the Killer?

—JERRY LEE LEWIS, to his wife's sister; Lewis
was under investigation for the suspicious death
of his young wife, Shawn; no charges were ever
brought against him

No trick or treaters came to my house for Halloween. For some reason, people around here are scared of me.

—GLENN DANZIG, formerly of the hard-core
band The Misfits

I think I might have been a bloody good Hitler. I'd be an excellent dictator. Very eccentric and quite mad.

—DAVID BOWIE, 1976

If I'd have made the army, we wouldn't have had all that trouble in Vietnam, 'cause I would have won it in a year.

—TED NUGENT

I may say a lot of strange and incomprehensible things as far as other people are concerned, but that is the way of all brilliance.

—TERENCE TRENT D'ARBY

My aspiration is to stand alone, to put myself on a pedestal and to hate myself for standing on a pedestal.

—DAVE PIRNER, of Soul Asylum, 1995

I want to be God, really. I want to be responsible for everything. I know it's fucking mad. I smoke spliff [marijuana] from when I get up to when I go to bed, so I put it down to that.

—TRICKY, 1995

Who knows? Maybe I'm insane, too, it runs in my family, but I always had a repulsive sort of need to be something more than human. I felt very puny as a human. I thought, "Fuck that. I want to be a Superman."

—DAVID BOWIE, 1976

Offstage, I'm Ozzie Nelson. I'm gentle. I walk around eating cookies and milk—well, cookies and beer. I work in opposites. Offstage I'm pretty nonviolent. I'm stable.

—ALICE COOPER, 1973

Every single human being alive is kinda weird, and when you put them under a magnifying glass, those little weirdnesses might become magnified and seem even . . . weirder. . . . I don't think I'm weird at all. I think I'm one of the most level-headed, grounded people in my life, and that's a fairly objective opinion, you know.

—MICHAEL STIPE, of R.E.M., 1995

259

People tell me I live in my own little world. I tell them, "Well, at least they know me there." —DAVID LEE ROTH

There are three layers to me. The first is alert, amiable, and at ease with the world. Then there is the sad, small boy. In all, there is this instinctive and at times aggressive character. I fluctuate between the three, but the stranger, the third layer only comes out in the music.
—PETER GABRIEL

There's nothing butch about me. See, that's the big myth, you know—the "loudmouthed American." I am the loudmouthed American—no one can be meaner, and no one can be more of a cunt than I am. But I don't want to be. It's a front, you know? I just do what I do to get what I have to get.
—CHRISSIE HYNDE, of the Pretenders, 1980

I never have a realistic sense of self. I either think everything I do is terrible and I'm the worst guy on the planet, or from time to time I'll think I'm the greatest gift to music and the coolest guy who ever lived, but that happens maybe an hour out of the week. Some days I'm more concerned with how my hair looks than what my guitar sounds like.
—DAVE NAVARRO, of Red Hot Chili Peppers, 1995

It's difficult analyzing yourself; it's easier having others do it for you. —MICK JAGGER, 1987

I became Ziggy Stardust. David Bowie went totally out the window. Everybody was convincing me that I was a Messiah.
—DAVID BOWIE, 1976

No. I'm not the Beatles. I'm me.
—JOHN LENNON (1940–1980), 1971

I'm not Led Zeppelin. I'm just this character who keeps saying, "I'm not Led Zeppelin." —ROBERT PLANT

I thought I was the greatest band in the world.
—JIMMY PAGE, of Led Zeppelin

I just don't have the time to sit around and think about *me* anymore. —BILLY JOEL, 1980

It's not easy living up to Janis Joplin, you know.
—JANIS JOPLIN (1943–1970)

> I look at what's there. What's there is legs and hair. —TINA TURNER

I don't think you ever lose the feeling of ugliness once you've had it. I feel better now than I ever have as far as my worth goes. But still . . . when I'm first in contact with people, I tend to get almost angry with them in a way because they're too stupid to see that I'm awful! —TANYA DONELLY, of Belly, 1994

As an adolescent, I was painfully shy, withdrawn. I didn't really have the nerve to sing my songs onstage, and nobody else was going to do them. I decided to do them in disguise so that I didn't have to actually go through the humiliation of going onstage and being myself. I continued designing characters with their own complete personalities and environments. I put them into interviews with me! Rather than be me—which I thought must be incredibly boring to anyone—I'd take Ziggy in, or Aladdin Sane or the Thin White Duke. It was a very strange thing to do.
—DAVID BOWIE, 1983

I thought it was only a matter of time before people discovered that I'm not as good as they thought and then no one would ever want me to be in their band again. —DAVE NAVARRO, of Red Hot Chili Peppers, 1995

I've grown up a lot in the last ten years. I've learned many lessons the hard way. My feet are on the ground now. I think fame and this business bring out the worst elements of your personality; they bring out the demons. These days I'm just a lot more comfortable with myself—with my sexuality, with my body, with my mind. . . . Things just don't bother me like they used to. Sometimes I feel like a moving camera, I'm constantly moving around myself and observing myself, critiquing myself. I'm aware of myself in a lot of ways that I never was before.   —BOY GEORGE, 1996

God, I'm glad I'm not me.

—BOB DYLAN

I know exactly what I'm about. There are people who innovate, people like [my father] Woody, but I'm not one of those. I'm just a guy who substantiates what the innovators do. I'm just a link between what went before and what's gonna be . . . and I'm honored as hell just to be a link in the chain, just to be part of the tradition.   —ARLO GUTHRIE, 1977

I'm not just a singer, or a dancer, or a performer. I want to be a lot of different things. People don't know what Bobby Brown is. I want to be mysterious. I don't want people to label me. I just wanna be Bobby, the Man Who Does Everything.

—BOBBY BROWN, 1989

I don't want to sound shallow, but I don't have any aspirations like someday I want to be a fucking president or actor. I'm a one-trick pony.   —SLASH, of Guns N' Roses, 1995

I'd like to end up sort of unforgettable.

—RINGO STARR

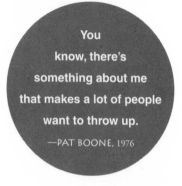

You know, there's something about me that makes a lot of people want to throw up.

—PAT BOONE, 1976

It's actually come as quite a shock to learn just how many people don't like me. —PHIL COLLINS

I'm a rebel with a lot of causes, and one of them is that I don't think I get enough respect. —RICK JAMES

I don't, contrary to popular opinion, take myself so seriously that I can't see the jokes. —STING, 1991

I suppose to most people I'm probably seen as an amiable idiot . . . a genial twit. I think I must be a victim of circumstance, really. Most of it's me own doing. I'm a victim of me own practical jokes.
—KEITH MOON (1946–1978),
of the Who, 1971

How can you think you're better than somebody else? I mean, I do certain things that millions of kids out there will never get to see or do, but I shouldn't think I'm better than them. We're all human.
—MICHAEL JACKSON, 1989

I think it's a good, humbling experience to scrub behind your own toilet. —NATALIE MERCHANT, 1995

Are you kidding? The world don't need me. Christ, I'm only five feet ten. —BOB DYLAN

I am not a leader. Neither your nor anyone else's. I am a rock musician, a mirror. You see yourself when you see the Who.
—PETE TOWNSHEND

People should realize, we are just jerks like them.
—BONO

As Ice Cube said, "Do I look like a fucking role model?"
—MICHAEL STIPE, of R.E.M.

I am not a saint. I am a noise. —JOAN BAEZ

Getting Older

<u>when i'm sixty-four</u>

etting old is a fascinating thing. The older you get, the older you want to get.
—KEITH RICHARDS

I'd rather have ten years of super-hypermost than live to be 70 by sitting in some goddamn chair watching TV.
—JANIS JOPLIN (1943–1970)

Yeah, you know people get wrinkled and gray because life beats the hell out of them. If life were all wonderful and every dream came true you wouldn't go gray, know what I mean?
—CHRIS ISAAK, 1995

People have this obsession: They want you to be like you were in 1969. They want you to, because otherwise their youth goes with you, you know?
—MICK JAGGER

So much of what I hear on the radio is boring. I think part of the reason is because it's not real. It may be real—maybe—if you're 18, but not if you're 30. People 30 years old wonder why they're not getting off on popular music the way they once did, and it's because nobody's singing for them. When you reach a certain age you're not naive anymore. Everything I write can't be a philosophical truth, but it certainly isn't innocent—because I'm not.
—PAUL SIMON, 1975

If it's too loud, you're too old.　　—TED NUGENT

Age makes no difference with music.
—NEIL YOUNG, 1995

I often wonder if the people who were into R.E.M. and Hüsker Dü and the Replacements seven years ago still like any of us. . . . That music was documenting those years, the early 20s of all of our lives. The people who were listening then, they were our age. Now they're in their late 20s and early 30s. . . . You had people nine years ago coming to the show with skateboards. Are they in suits now, and do they still enjoy the music and know why it's good, and why it was good for them then?
—BOB MOULD,
of Hüsker Dü, 1989

> I didn't think I'd get to be 40, to tell you the truth. Jeez, I feel like I'm a hundred million years old.
> —JERRY GARCIA (1942–1995), of the Grateful Dead, 1991

I'm just so happy to still be here and have a career at 48. . . . I never thought I'd be here. I thought I'd have a run and it would have been a good one and I'd be down in Florida fishing and reminiscing.
—JIMMY BUFFET, 1995

A lot of people try to disguise the fact, like 40's the threshold of middle age. I say, "Hey, I'm 40 and I'm proud!" Why not? We're the biggest generation in history and we're all getting older. It doesn't mean anything any more. I just feel in the prime of my life. Why shouldn't I crow about it?
—STING, 1991

I used to be afraid of being in my 40s. Now I find out my 40s are pretty good. Of course, I'm rich and I'm married to Christie Brinkley. And that will tend to skew one's view of things.
—BILLY JOEL; Billy Joel and Christie Brinkley
have since divorced; 1993

Hey, man, I'm new with every song I sing. As we get older, we feel the need for newness. I'm going to be 45, but I'm still feeling new and amazed by the world I live in.

—STEVIE WONDER, 1995

Well, I'm 44 years old. I have two children. . . . I think it's amazing I'm *here*. Today, I think it's incredible, after burying two band members and giving birth to two children in the past 15 years and running this band, that I can even be bothered to go out and do a show.

—CHRISSIE HYNDE, of the Pretenders, 1996

I don't know whether I'll reach 40. I don't know whether I'll reach 35. I can't be sure about that. I am bloody serious. I didn't think I'd make 30.

—JIMMY PAGE, of Led Zeppelin

I'm 67, and I'm being accepted by the MTV crowd!

—TONY BENNETT

I want to do this till I'm old and little. I'd like to be like John Lee Hooker: all in my little suit, with my little gut hanging out, playing music, strumming my guitar. I know I want that.

—LENNY KRAVITZ, 1995

You know, I hope I never forget that incredible time of evolving from a girl into a woman. You start wearing hair curlers, and your breasts are growing, and you're climbing up into some tree to kiss some boy. . . . It's so important to always keep that innocence.

—RICKI LEE JONES, 1979

And I've always been the ages of three, 75, and 12 all at the same time. As a baby, I was very old, and in my 20s I was very young. It's strange how it seems that you contain all of the people you are and were and will be.

—JONI MITCHELL, 1988

I might be just 26, but I'm an old woman in disguise.

—ARETHA FRANKLIN, 1968

Without reservation, I think it's very important for youth to have anger and an awareness of the nowness. I think all those things are part and parcel of being young. But I think that's just a passing grace, and then you shift to another viewpoint in life that's tempered by experiences, and the future becomes very important. But you need all the rest, that vortex of mess and misbehavior, to then straighten up and see where the future can go.

—DAVID BOWIE, 1983

I've certainly been really difficult in the past, in a lot of ways, or extremely temperamental. But that's because I was beset, and I didn't have it together. It's a different story now. Of course, I'm older. Supposedly when you get older, you get something from all of it before, or you drop dead and that's the end of it.

—LOU REED, 1989

I don't wear a corset, I don't wear a wig, I don't lie about my age, or sing songs about dating girls after high school. I'm an adult.

—STING

I'm finally starting to grow up and cope with life, which is a difficult, complicated affair at best.

—T-BONE BURNETT, 1983

I don't really feel like I've grown up. . . . Most of the time I just feel like a sort of weird little girl. Yeah, a weird, demented sort of female girl-freak.

—NENEH CHERRY, 1989

I think the transition from boy to man has taken me, probably, about two and a half years. I am actually a man now, whereas six months ago, or three months ago, or even two months ago, I was probably still verging on boy.

—ROLAND GIFT, of Fine Young Cannibals, 1989

it's the end of the world as we know it

t's funny the way most people love the dead. . . . Once you are dead you are made for life. —JIMI HENDRIX (1942–1970), 1968

Well, some people die and some people are survivors. I'm a survivor.
—JANIS JOPLIN (1943–1970)

It's such an enormous concept. Death! What is any story telling about? What are myths about? It's all about dealing with death. Something that we can't understand, that we can't quite grasp, that really terrifies us. . . . Everything is about that. Sex is about death!
—STING, 1991

We spend our whole lives in this little cage of consciousness, in this bubble of consciousness, but you realize that one day this won't be there—this whole reference point from which you've seen things that you call ME. It's gonna go. —ROBYN HITCHCOCK, 1995

Death is death, and the ego can't handle the consequences. We should all struggle to the last to hold on to life. . . . I'm gonna claw, scratch, bite, kick, and kill if I have to in order to stay alive.
—BILLY JOEL, 1982

I'm not afraid of death. That is the greatest mystery of all.
—JIMMY PAGE, of Led Zeppelin, 1975

I took the job [as a grave digger] because I thought it'd help me overcome my fear of death. When I first went on the job the other guys in the cemetery initiated me by putting me in a coffin and

271

closing the lid. That scared the shit out of me—but I've had no fear of death since! It cured me. —ROD STEWART, 1988

It's always been my ambition to be killed by some lover in a fit of passionate jealousy. —MARIANNE FAITHFUL

When I die, bury me on my stomach and let the world kiss my ass. —L. L. COOL J

I want to be buried in an unmarked grave. —BOB DYLAN

On my gravestone, I want it to say, "I told you I was sick." —TOM WAITS

When I die I want people just to play my music, go wild, freak out, do anything they want to do. Enjoy themselves. —JIMI HENDRIX (1942–1970)

I left a trail. When I'm gone, I won't be gone. Like Muddy Waters, you don't see him, but he lives on. That's the way it will be with me. . . . As generation and generation go by, they can say, "I heard of John Lee Hooker, oh, yes. I never seen the man, but I would have liked to have seen him." —JOHN LEE HOOKER, 1989

I've been closer to death a few more times than a lot of people. And what I've found out is that whatever it is [beyond death], it's worth waiting for. —KEITH RICHARDS

I don't think there's anything else in life apart from a near-death experience that shows you how extensive the mind is. —JERRY GARCIA (1942–1995), of the Grateful Dead

I recommend everybody come close to death. You don't worry about anything after that. —CHRIS STEIN, of Blondie, who suffered from a nearly fatal skin disease, 1986

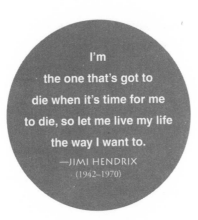

I'm
the one that's got to
die when it's time for me
to die, so let me live my life
the way I want to.
—JIMI HENDRIX
(1942–1970)

You know, there's a big lie in this business. The lie is that it's okay to go out in flames. But that doesn't do anybody much good. I may be wrong, but I think [Jimi] Hendrix was trying to come around. I think he had gotten a glimpse of what he needed to change, and that he really wanted to change. And I found myself in a similar position. Some of us can be examples about going ahead and growing, and some of us, unfortunately, don't make it there, and end up being examples because they had to die. I hit rock bottom, but thank God my bottom wasn't death.

—STEVIE RAY VAUGHN (1954–1990);
Stevie Ray Vaughn died in a helicopter crash
after finally becoming clean and sober

I'm not trying to kill myself, that's silly. I have a lust for life; I wouldn't be doing this if I didn't really like seeing new places and doing new things. I love the idea of life, yet I have this other self, and he goes up there and makes fun of death.

—ALICE COOPER, 1973

I'd rather kill myself. . . . I'm not going to be around to witness my artistic decline. —ELVIS COSTELLO

I'd rather be dead than singing "Satisfaction" when I'm 45.

—MICK JAGGER

I've got this death wish; I don't like life.

—ERIC CLAPTON, 1974

The American public really does have a death wish for me. They want me to die. I'm not going to die.

—COURTNEY LOVE, of Hole, 1995

I can fulfill most of my dreams here. Even if I have a death wish, there's a convenient platform from which to hurtle to one's doom, flying meself headlong, perhaps even commit sooey-side amidst the glorious Surrey country side. —KEITH MOON (1946–1978), of the Who, musing about his house in Surrey (Moon overdosed on anti-alcoholism tablets)

I found out through the Internet that I have AIDS. I learned I was dead. . . . I was in San Francisco at Lollapalooza, and this girl walked up to me and stopped like she'd seen a ghost. And she said, "You're not dead." And I said, "No, you're right. Wow."

—LAYNE STALEY, of Alice in Chains, on the wild rumors circulating about him, 1996

The only reason you cry when someone dies is because you know how beautiful it's been and you know you're going to miss that emotion. —STEVIE WONDER

There's nothing to say, really. It happens every day in America. Dysfunction, drugs—it was compounded by the fame, but it's nothing romantic. It's just tragic. It's real emotional pain, and it's nobody's business. Who cares? —KRIST NOVOSELIC, of Nirvana, on Kurt Cobain's suicide, 1996

I'm not condoning what he did. But you at least have to respect him. I think suicide is pretty wasteful. But sometimes people have to do the most drastic thing in the world to let people know that there's something wrong. —PATRICK, of Filter, on Kurt Cobain's suicide, 1995

[Kurt Cobain's] death is nothing I really talk about because I just think it trivializes the whole thing. It gets turned into a cultural comment. I try not to forget that there's a real human being behind all that cultural talk. I think it's pretty amazing that somebody in such a short life could cause so much trouble and talk.

—BILLY CORGAN, of the Smashing Pumpkins, 1995

I thought [Jim Morrison] would never die. I thought he'd outlive everybody, like one of those Irish drunks who drink a fifth of whisky a day and live until they're 80. He seemed invulnerable, the way he would do things like jump out of windows without getting hurt. . . . I still think about him quite a bit. I always have dreams that he's still alive, and we're playing together. Wishful thinking.

—ROBBY KRIEGER, of the Doors, 1994

I tend to take death fairly matter of factly. There is absolutely nothing you can do about it. I try to be strong for people who are more emotional about it. On the other hand, Jerry [Garcia] was pretty much my best friend, so it's not a particularly easy loss for me. But I have a torch to carry here. To spend a lot of time moping and grieving seems way beside the point to me. I'm doing what I believe he would have me doing: bringing music to people.

—BOB WEIR, of the Grateful Dead, 1996

Elvis died the day he went into the army.

—JOHN LENNON (1940–1980), responding
to the news that Elvis Presley had died

If there were any illusions left at all for the children of the '60s, they too died Monday night—when the music died.

—*Time*, on the death of John Lennon, 1980

Like the Kennedys and King . . . except this time there was a difference. This time someone crawled out of a dark place, lifted a gun, and killed an artist. This was something new. This time, someone murdered a song.

—*New York* magazine, on John Lennon's
death, 1980

sources

Books

Aquila, Richard. *The Old Time Rock & Roll: A Chronicle of an Era (1954–1963)*. New York: Macmillan, 1989.

Bangs, Lester. *Psychotic Reactions and Carburetor Dung*. New York: Vintage, 1987.

Buchanan, Scott. *Rock 'n' Roll: The Famous Lyrics*. New York: HarperCollins, 1974.

Dannen, Fredric. *Hit Men: Power Brokers and Fast Money Inside the Music Business*. New York: Random House, 1990.

Davis, Francis. *The History of the Blues*. New York: Hyperion, 1995.

Evans, Liz. *Women, Sex and Rock 'n' Roll*. New York: HarperCollins, 1994.

Freeman, Robert. *The Beatles*. New York: Barnes & Noble Books.

Friedlander, Paul. *Rock and Roll: A Social History*. New York: HarperCollins, 1996.

Frith, Simon. *Facing the Music*. New York: Pantheon, 1988.

Garr, Gillian. *She's a Rebel: The History of Women in Rock & Roll*. Seattle: Seal Press, 1992.

Gillett, Charlie. *The Sound of the City: The Rise of Rock and Roll*. New York: Da Capo Press, 1996.

Goldman, Albert. *Elvis*. New York: McGraw-Hill, 1981.

Goldman, Albert. *Sound Bites*. New York: Random House, 1992.

Guralnik, Peter. *Sweet Soul Music*. New York: HarperCollins, 1986.

Henke, James, and James George-Warren. *The Rolling Stone Illustrated History of Rock & Roll.* New York: Random House, 1992.

Henry, Tricia. *Break All Rules: Punk Rock and the Making of a Style.* Ann Arbor: University of Michigan Press, 1989.

Huxley, Martin. *Aerosmith: The Fall and Rise of Rock's Great Band.* New York: St. Martin's Press, 1995.

Loder, Kurt. *Bat Chain Puller: Rock & Roll in the Age of Celebrity.* New York: St. Martin's Press, 1990.

Marre, Jeremy, and Hannah Charlton. *Beats of the Heart: Popular Music of the World.* New York: Pantheon Books, 1985.

Marsh, Dave. *Rock & Roll Confidential Report.* New York: Pantheon Books, 1985.

Marsh, Dave. *The New Book of Rock Lists.* New York: Simon & Schuster, 1994.

O'Brien, Lucy. *Shebop: The Definitive History of Women in Rock, Pop and Soul.* New York: Penguin Books, 1995.

Pareles, Jon, and Patricia Romanowski. *The Rolling Stone Encyclopedia of Rock & Roll.* New York: Summit Books, 1983.

Patoski, Joe Nick, and Bill Crawford. *Soul to Soul: The Stevie Ray Vaughn Story.* Boston: Little, Brown, 1993.

Riley, Tim. *Hard Rain: A Dylan Commentary.* New York: Knopf, 1992.

Rolling Stone Press Staff. *Rolling Stone: 25 Years of Journalism on the Edge.* New York: Doubleday, 1993.

Toop, David. *Rap Attack 2: African Rap to Global Hip Hop.* London: Pluto Press, 1994.

Vicent, Rickey. *Funk: The Music, the People, and the Rhythm of the One.* New York: St. Martin's Press, 1996.

Wenner, Jann S. *Twenty Years of Rolling Stone: What a Long Strange Trip It's Been.* New York: Straight Arrow Publishers, 1987.

White, Timothy. *Rock Lives: Profiles and Interviews.* New York: Henry Holt, 1990.

Wolff, Daniel. *You Send Me: The Life and Times of Sam Cooke.* New York: Quill, 1995.

Magazines and Newspapers

Alternative Press

Bikini

Classic Rock

Details

Entertainment Weekly

Guitar Player

Huh

I-D

Life

Los Angeles Times

Mean Street

Musician

Newsweek

People

Playboy

Pulse

Rolling Stone

The Source

Spin

Time

Urb

Us

Vanity Fair

Vibe

Television

Rock & Roll. Executive producer, Elizabeth Deane. Ten-part series. PBS. KCET, Los Angeles. September 26–29, 1995.